MW01075274

One Hairy Knee

One Hairy Knee

Amy Arndt

PIGEON GIRL
PRESS

Copyright © 2020 Amy Arndt.

All rights reserved. No part of this book may be reproduced, stored, or
transmitted by any means—whether auditory, graphic, mechanical, or
electronic—without written permission of both publisher and author, except
in the case of brief excerpts used in critical articles and reviews. Unauthorized
reproduction of any part of this work is illegal and is punishable by law.

Cover design by Drue Wagner

978-1-7341299-9-1 - Paperback
978-1-7341299-1-5 - eBook

Library of Congress Control Number: 2019917380

For Tim, Matthew, Stephanie, and Emily Rose

Contents

Introduction - The El Paso Test

When I was a kid, my stepfather James would evaluate a person by putting them through what I like to call "The El Paso Test." The test is based on whether or not you would ride to El Paso with a person, because for our family, driving to El Paso offered 12 hours of a whole lot of nothing to see. If you're in a car with anyone for that long, it gets intimate pretty quickly. You'll observe how that person eats. You'll learn if they bite their nails. You'll smell their smells. They'll tell you all about their pets, their childhood, their second cousins. By the end of the journey, you'll know almost everything about each other. The interesting thing about this method is that you don't even have to have a conversation with the person before figuring out whether they would make the cut. Somehow, you just *know*.

James is an artist, so we took a lot of family trips to art museums. We would sit on the benches in the galleries, looking at the art on the wall, and James would spot someone, lean in to me, and whisper,

"I'd ride to El Paso with her."

It might sound creepy, but James doesn't have a creepy bone in his body. He would want to ride to El Paso with the stranger he was talking about because that person probably had dreadlocks or cool tattoos or was otherwise unique. You generally didn't want to ride to El Paso with Plain Janes, ordinary Joes, or your regular everyday accountant. Unless, of course, the regular everyday accountant had some great stories to tell.

Once I got married and had children, my husband Tim and I put a spin on this unusual family tradition and used it to compare two people. My favorite comparison is two politicians. For example:

"Hey, Tim. Would you rather ride to El Paso with Donald Trump or Ted Cruz?"

"I'd rather stay home and steam vegetables," Tim says. He can't bear to choose.

I'm constantly thinking up scenarios of which person would be a better El Paso companion. There are the ones that are hard to decide because they would both be fun: Willie Nelson or Bob Dylan? Jimmy Fallon or Jimmy Kimmel? Ruth Bader Ginsburg or Michelle Obama? Then there are the ones that would be hard to choose because both options are terrible. Vladimir Putin or Kim Jung-un? Ann Coulter or Sarah Palin? The stranger with extreme body odor or the really gassy one?

For the record, I would totally pick Sarah Palin. Something about her reminds me of a boss I used to have who was as country as creamed corn, but her down-home ways of discussing things tickled me, because I'm still a small town girl at heart myself. Plus, if I had Ann Coulter in my car for longer than about ten minutes, there's no guarantee I wouldn't open the door and push her out.

I've spent my entire life with a boatload of family and friends who pass the El Paso test. I also have a small boatful of people in my life that I'd prefer to just meet in El Paso and see a few times a year. Those are my "small dose" people. We all have them. And then, there are the Ann Coulters of the world. I've learned that those are the kind of people with whom I couldn't bear to ride in the car to our neighborhood grocery a block away from home.

Lucky for me, the people closest to me are people with whom a trip to El Paso would be an absolute hoot. The list is long and full of delightful relatives and friends. This book is for those people.

It's also for Al Roker.

The Greeting

My story begins in Bowie, Texas, a tiny little town northwest of Dallas where both of my parents grew up. In 1950, shortly after they were born, Bowie's population was 4,544, and as of the 2010 Census, it was barely over 5,200, so I think based on that we can all agree that people aren't exactly lining up to move there. Yet two of the world's best families settled in Bowie - Dorothy and Glenn Underwood, my dad's parents, and Mabel and Mark High, my mom's parents. The Underwoods and Highs had a lot more than Bowie in common. Grandpa Glenn and Grandpa Mark both owned blue-collar businesses in Bowie. Both families were United Methodists, except for Grandpa Glenn, who wasn't fond of church because he couldn't stand people who acted holy on Sunday then spent the next six days sinning. Granny Dorothy and Grandma Mabel were both women who grew up poor but managed to be extraordinarily glamorous. They dressed beautifully and knew how to properly accessorize. For many years, all of my grandparents smoked inside their houses, and the combination of the smell of smoke, bacon, and Estée Lauder perfume was really comforting and pleasing to me.

My mom, Judy Kaye High, and my dad, Glenn Eldon Underwood, Jr., were in the Bowie High School band, and every year, the band put on the Bowie Band Show, a fundraiser and talent revue of sorts where the parents did performances to raise money for things the school wouldn't pay for, like band uniforms and instruments. The moms were called "The Red Hot Mamas," and the dads were "The Cool, Cool Papas." One year, Granny and Grandma and the other Red Hot Mamas dressed in overalls and sang some kind of corny farm song on stage. At the end of the skit, the schtick was that Grandma Mabel would throw out the contents of a slop bucket out into the audience. (For you more sophisticated types, that's a bedpan.) They filled the bucket with a pile of yellow confetti intended to look like urine, and when Grandma tossed the bucket, instead of the contents spreading out, the entire bucket of confetti urine landed in the front row, directly on top of Dr. Hulen Crumpler's head.

It wasn't fake urine pranks every day in Bowie, though. In November of 1963, Mom had been dating a boy named Larry for six months when they were in a terrible car accident together. Mom was injured and hospitalized, and Larry tragically didn't survive. Then, in May of 1964, my grandfather Mark went missing. Mark was an engaged and respected community member, former mayor of Bowie, and owner of Wichita Construction Company. Friends and family began an extensive search, and law enforcement ordered an airplane to broaden the search to larger rural areas. Several days later, an oil company agent contacted the County Sheriff to report that he saw a car resembling Mark's parked on a county road outside of town. When law enforcement arrived, they found Mark dead inside the car. The death was ruled a suicide.

To help the family, the Bowie High School band director Jack Willbanks, an all-around great guy, approached Grandma Mabel before Mom's senior year and suggested that Mom become a majorette to give her something to fill her time. If you're not a Texan, a majorette is a baton-twirler who accompanies the band with routines. Mom, an accomplished musician but not a dancer, enrolled in private baton-twirling lessons, and somehow made it through the audition. In an unusual form of therapy, Mom was able to distract herself from her two major life traumas by being a Bowie High School Band majorette.

Jack Willbanks may have been a kind man with good intentions, but he was also pretty brave to assume the risk of allowing an inexperienced baton-twirler to perform with the Bowie Band. At one of the pep rallies in the gym, Mom got a little ambitious hurling her baton around, and she konked herself in the head. Not one to stop in the middle of a performance, Mom made it all the way through and was standing courtside after the performance when a fellow majorette pointed out that Mom's head was bleeding. It was only then that it was determined that somehow, Mom had knocked herself nearly unconscious with her baton, yet had managed to complete the routine without missing a step. The woman is a legend.

Several months after Larry died, Mom started dating my dad. Dad was everything Mom needed at the time because he was responsible, reliable, and safe. Dad was a drummer in a band, and wore dark horn-rimmed Buddy Holly glasses. He came from a solid family, and Mom and Dad's parents knew each other well.

Mom was a year ahead of Dad in school, so when she graduated from high school in 1965, she set off to Texas Tech University in Lubbock, Texas to major in elementary education. "Why elementary education?" I asked.

"I had no clue," said Mom.

Considering what Mom had been through, she struggled to navigate college, instead devoting ample time to dancing the Mashed Potato to the Rolling Stones and partying.

She did pretty well her first semester but quite poorly her second, so she returned to Bowie to live at home with Grandma Mabel. She applied to nursing school and helped redecorate Grandma's house while Grandma grieved.

Dad finished his senior year of high school in Bowie, graduating valedictorian, and was accepted to the University of Texas at Austin. In the summer of 1966, Dad was supposed to be attending Freshman Orientation, but instead, he was in the Bowie Hospital with a severe case of mono. On August 1, 1966, Dad woke up and looked at the hospital room television to see smoke coming off the UT tower. The smoke was from the handgun fire from the Austin police officers attempting to hit or obstruct 25-year old Charles Whitman, who murdered his wife and mother in the middle of the night, then climbed up the main tower building at UT and began shooting. When it was over, Whitman had killed 16 people and injured 31 others. Had Dad not been sick that summer, he could very possibly have been walking across the campus at the time of the shooting.

Dad recovered from mono and made it to business school at UT, and Mom moved to Austin to attend a year of nursing school at Brackenridge Hospital. Mom and Dad got engaged, married in Bowie after Dad's sophomore year, and returned to Austin where they moved into UT's married student housing. Mom got a job working in labor and delivery at Brackenridge, and Dad worked at the University Co-Op as a cashier until he graduated.

While Dad was at UT, the Nixon administration initiated a draft to add more troops to the Vietnam War. At the time, male college students were granted annual deferments as long as they maintained good academic standing. Dad certainly maintained good academic standing, but when his senior year started in the fall of 1969, educational deferments were cancelled.

On December 1, 1969, a draft lottery was held on national television. Slips of paper representing 366 days of the year (including February 29, as it was a leap year) were placed in plastic capsules. The capsules were mixed in a shoebox and dumped into a deep glass jar. All 366 numbers were drawn and the order was documented on a board, and each county in the country used that birth order to select draftees.

The evening of the televised draft, Dad was at work at the Co-Op. When he got back home that evening, he turned on the tv, and they were already at #150.

"I remember thinking *nobody* would be so unlucky to go in the first 150," Dad says.

He saw about 100 numbers get called, then went to bed thinking surely he was "safe." The next morning when Dad went to campus for class, he picked up a copy of UT's school newspaper, *The Daily Texan*, and looked for his birthday.

Dad's birthday, September 7, was the 8th number drawn.

"First time I ever won anything!" Dad said. He then made a really hilarious Dad joke about how he could take me to the exact spot where he read it because that's where he pooped his pants.

Jokes aside, I can't imagine how terrifying that moment must have been for those young men. I've watched footage of the 1969 draft and when my Dad's number was pulled, it took my breath away and I cried. I thought about what Dorothy and Glenn and so many parents must have felt when they realized their son was headed to war. I think about what Mom felt, a young newlywed with a husband going to Vietnam. Most of all, I think about what my Dad felt when he saw his number listed.

With help from the woman who ran the Montague County draft board, Dad got permission to finish school and graduate on May 30, 1970, and was scheduled to enter the Army in October of the same year.

In September of 1970, Dad's letter arrived. The letters sent to the inductees were the most sterile of form letters one can possibly imagine. At the top of the letter it read, "Selective Service System. Order to Report for Induction." The letter was addressed from The President of the United States to the draftee. The body of the letter started with a simple salutation:

GREETING:

Not "greetings," just the word greeting, followed by a colon. Then it cut right to the chase.

"You are hereby ordered to report for induction to the Armed Forces of the United States, and to report at (place) on (date) at (time) for forwarding to an Armed Forces Induction Station." For Dad, that was the bus station in Bowie, Texas on 14 Oct 1970 at 5:00 AM.

That was that. The letter was signed by the local draft board clerk. No, "best wishes" or "thank you for what you're about to get into" or "peace out." From there, there was a lot of fine print about how if you didn't follow the instructions and report for induction, you'd go to federal prison.

The morning Dad reported, he was the only person who showed up because nobody else from Bowie was called in that group. The woman who ran the draft board told Dad that the bus was bound for Dallas that day (about a 90 minute drive), and she gave Dad instructions on how to walk to the Dallas Induction Center from the bus station. Dad made it on time to the Induction Center, where he underwent an intense full day of physical exams and questions, then Dad and hundreds of other young men got on a plane and flew to Los Angeles to start six weeks of Basic Training at Fort Ord, California.

Dad loves to tell basic training stories, and how he returned a shadow of himself after spending time in Austin drinking beer and eating everything in sight. At Basic Training, Dad was called "the old man," since almost all of the guys in his company were 17 or 18 years old, fresh out of high school. Dad was 23.

Dad entered the Army with three key things going for him. He had extremely poor vision from the time he was a small child. He also entered the Army already knowing how to type 40 words a minute. Finally, Dad is highly intelligent and an all-around responsible guy. Due to Dad's poor vision, they didn't want him shooting the wrong guys, and because he could type, he would be better served doing desk work. Though Dad was drawn 8th in the draft to go to Vietnam, his special circumstances kept him from going to battle. If you ask me, that's when Dad really won something.

After Basic Training, Dad was ordered to report to Fort Huachuca, Arizona, where he did a variety of desk jobs and thanked his lucky stars he wasn't on the battlefield. Mom went to Arizona to live with Dad, and since there was a war going on and there wasn't available housing on base, they were given a stipend to live off base. Mom and Dad found a little trailer with what Mom describes as "a little shanty of a bedroom built onto it."

Mom and Dad were eager to start a family, but Mom was struggling to get pregnant. First, she was diagnosed with endometriosis. Then, the doctor found a mass on Mom's ovary and was unsure whether it was benign or malignant, so the situation required surgery. The same day Mom's surgery was scheduled, Dad got orders to go to Korea. But once again, luck kicked in, and Mom's surgery canceled Dad's orders. Mom's mass was benign, and thanks to that ridiculously serendipitous situation, I was conceived in the little trailer, which tickles me and keeps me somewhat humble. To add to Dad's series of good-luck moments, during the middle of Mom's pregnancy, Dad got released early, since the Vietnam withdrawal was happening.

Mom and Dad moved back to Austin to finish waiting for me to arrive, and Dad landed a job working at the Water Development

Board in downtown Austin. Because Dad had just gotten out of the Army, his new job's insurance wouldn't cover the cost of my birth. Thanks to Mom's connections at Brackenridge Hospital, they were able to work out a payment plan for the hospital fee, and secured a private room at the charge of a semi-private room. They even let Mom bring her own supplies so they wouldn't be charged inflated hospital prices for the things you could easily bring from home. When the final bill was posted, I cost Mom and Dad a whopping $500. I was financed through monthly payments of $50. Dad and Mom both tell me I was worth every penny.

My dad, Glenn Underwood, greeting my Granny Dorothy Underwood (center) and my Grandma Mabel High (left) at Austin's Brackenridge Hospital on October 2, 1972, the day of my birth. Grandma must have been so excited that she forgot to take off her sunglasses, so she's standing outside the hospital nursery looking like Roy Orbison.

Come Here, Kids!

I'm hardly an expert on child development, but I'm fairly certain babies can be divided into two camps: the babies who walk early and struggle with verbal skills, and the babies who talk early and struggle to walk.

I was the talking kind of baby. It took me forever and a day to learn how to walk, to the point where my parents were pretty concerned. Dad used to laugh about it and say, "Do you think they'll let her have her Social Security checks if she's still not walking by then?" I took my first steps at 19 months, and according to Dad, one moment I was crawling, then the next moment, "The chase was on." I've kind of always been a "do it big or don't do it at all" kind of gal.

Thankfully I balanced out the walking part by talking pretty much the second I popped out of my mom's body. Mom would take me with her to the grocery, securing me in the baby-holding area of the shopping cart, and whenever I spotted children, I would dramatically grab my hands open and closed and yell, "Come here, kids!" Except since I was a baby, it came out in two words: "Commere, kids!"

I spent my first 4 ½ years as an only child. I was the first grandchild on my dad's side and the third on my mom's, so I got loads of attention. A typical first-time parent, Mom compiled stacks of photo albums with pictures of me being held by delighted family members, all labeled carefully with the date and a brief description of the occasion. There's an envelope with a lock of my hair from my first haircut that I've pondered selling on eBay to a person seeking a hair sample from 1973, because you know that person exists.

As a baby, I had a bit of an addiction to pacifiers. One day I threw my last one out of the car window and sent my parents into a mild panic. Another time when I was out of pacifiers, Dad went to the grocery store down the street and put a handful of them on the check-out counter.

"They keep me calm and help me sleep," he said sheepishly to the teenage girl at the counter.

Mom stayed at home with me, so when she wasn't entertaining me herself, I grew up on a solid '70s educational diet of *Sesame Street*, *Mr. Rogers*, and occasionally, *The Electric Company*. But let's face it, *The Electric Company* was by far the least desirable of those selections. It sounds like it's meant to teach little kids about public utility policies, because that would be so incredibly PBS, but it was actually developed to help kids with grammar and reading as only Morgan Freeman, Rita Moreno, and Mel Brooks could.

Overall, Mom wasn't a big fan of television outside of the PBS arena, so I also spent countless hours listening to music. Mom played the piano and Dad played the drums, and they would have awesome family music sessions where they'd play Beatles songs while I jammed out. I got really into music, especially vinyl. I'd sit on the carpet in our wood-paneled living room, listening to Stevie Wonder's *Songs in the Key of Life,* The Doobie Brothers' *Captain and Me,* and Willie Nelson's *Red Headed Stranger,* poring over the record covers, singing along to every song. Later in the '70s, I was so smitten with Herb Albert's album *Rise,* I drew some pretty awesome abstract representations of the songs on the album, and my Mom got so excited about it she mailed them to the record company. I'm kind of surprised I didn't get Picasso famous right then and there, but evidently the secretary at A&M Records took one look at my fabulous art, rolled her eyes and tossed them straight into the trash, lit up a Salem Light at her desk, and went on about her day.

When it came time to teach me to read, Mom developed a homemade version of *Hooked on Phonics* using cans of syrupy fruit salad and a box of toothpicks. One syllable words were rewarded with a piece of fruit that I could fish out with a toothpick. For two-syllable words, I could grab a maraschino cherry. By the time school started, I couldn't ride a bike, but I could read at a *Finnegans Wake* level.

Dad still worked at the Water Development Board in downtown Austin, and we lived out in the boondocks on the outskirts of town, which is now just known as Central Austin, which is just nutballs to my parents. Dad loves to tell me about how you used to be able to stand on the front porch and look out and see the Austin skyline miles away in the distance. If you stood on that front porch now, you'd see the blinding lights of one of about 15 fast food restaurant signs and very possibly a SWAT standoff.

Back then, the house cost $18,500, and the house payment was $150 a month. Now, houses on that street are worth 400K.

Dad carpooled to work with a man named Tommy. I have absolutely no recollection of what Tommy looked like, what his last name was, or if he even had a family. If you put me in a time machine and five guys walked into the room, and one of them was Tommy, I'd never in a million years be able to pick him out. But something about that guy got into my head, and so in the absence of a sibling, I created an imaginary friend, and I named him Tommy.

Now, if my imaginary friend Tommy walked into the room, *everybody* would know it was my Tommy. Tommy had red, white and blue hair, and his head was shaped like a football turned sideways (like Ernie, not Bert). He was three feet tall. We were very close, and I would have ridden to El Paso with Tommy in a heartbeat. Mainly because by all accounts (all of them mine), Tommy was an incredibly loyal guy who took direction very well. I was a super bossy kid from the minute I could boss people around, except since I didn't have anyone to boss around, Tommy got the brunt of it. Mom would walk in and hear me saying, "No, Tommy!" as I was sternly scolding Tommy for whatever sin he'd just committed.

Now that I'm a grown-up with kids of my own, my kids love it when I tell them about Tommy, because they understand that I was not your ordinary normal kid and they think Tommy stories are the funniest thing ever. Because of this, I have loads of Tommy drawings that the kids drew when they were little. The resemblance to Tommy is uncanny, I assure you.

35 year old Tommy

6 year old Amy underwood

Tommy (actual size) and a drawing of me wearing a gigantic Flavor Flav butterfly necklace. My age is inaccurate as Tommy left when I was 4 ½, but hey. Tommy and I both look mentally deranged, so I'm not sure what that's about. Drawing credit: Matthew Arndt (or at least we all took a vote and think so. Nobody's certain.).

As mentioned, I was rather spoiled, so instead of ignoring my highly unusual relationship with an imaginary 3-foot tall adult male with a misshapen head and tri-colored hair, my parents decided to play along. When Tommy needed extra help, Mom was up for the task. Tommy had a place setting at dinner. When it was time for my bath, Tommy joined me, and Mom toweled him off when bath time was over. I'm guessing when the pediatrician asked how things were going, Mom answered that I was fine, thanks, but conveniently forgot to mention I was bathing with an invisible adult male.

Tommy at bath time. I love his little robe and the bubble bath! Not weird at all that I bathed with an imaginary man. Drawing credit: Emily Rose Arndt.

Though I'd created my own friend to keep me company, I hated going outside to play. Most kids can't wait to go outside and run around and throw sticks and tackle other kids and ride things with wheels, but not this girl. Mom would tell me to go outside and I would stand there, baffled and lost. Within minutes, Mom would find me standing outside the screen door, staring inside. I don't know why she didn't rush me to the child psychologist. In the 70s, you just let your kids be weirdos.

Since we lived out past the city limits, our street was a bit countrified. We didn't have gutters or curbs, and we didn't have the benefits of all city services. Our backyards were connected to our next door neighbors' yards with chain link fences, giving us clear views into each other's worlds.

Dad tells a great story of our next door neighbor who allowed his adult daughter and son-in-law to move in with him.

"These idiots dug up half of his backyard and planted a vegetable garden, which they never touched again." Dad says, "His beautiful lawn became a huge weed patch overnight." (Dad keeps a pristine lawn, so this really irritated him.) One night, Mom and Dad woke up in the middle of the night to the sound of squealing. They woke to look out the window and discover a giant hog in a pen in the neighbor's yard, about 25 feet from our kitchen.

"I guess they thought if they moved him in in the middle of the night, we wouldn't notice it the next day?" Mom said, incensed. "I just thought, what happens when my little child puts her hand through the fence and has it bitten off by a 400 pound hog?" Mom forgot that her little child refused to go outside, but still, I see her point.

Dad went next door to confront the neighbor about the hog, and the neighbor said sorry, he didn't think they would get rid of it. Dad contacted Travis County, who informed him they could not keep hogs within 50 feet of our kitchen.

"Either they got rid of Miss Piggy, or county animal control would take the bacon," Dad said.

The neighbors sold the hog. Game point: Glenn Underwood.

With Mom and Dad's only child refusing to play outside and imagining up Tommy to keep her company, I'm sure they felt all kinds of pressure to have a second child. Finally, after a combination of medical miracles, Mom got pregnant a second time. Thanks to Mom's dedication to keeping my childhood photo albums organized, we have this fantastic photo:

Wow, I look deranged in this photo, so maybe that drawing of Tommy and me that Matthew drew isn't that far off. That, or I was rendered incapacitated at the shock of having so many presents to open. And is that Tommy dressed as Santa in the background? Very possibly.

Even though Mom had a shirt that said "Baby" with an arrow pointing to her stomach to state the obvious, the message didn't exactly sink in for me. When it came time for Mom and Dad to head to the hospital to have the baby, Dad sat me down to explain that I would be staying with family friends while the baby was born. This conversation caused me to completely lose my mind. I told friends that Mom and Dad were trading me in, and that I couldn't live with them any more. I mean, how in the world would I share my parents' attention with anyone besides Tommy?

Soon enough, I met my sister Emily, and as they say, it's a good thing babies are cute, because I fell for her right off the bat. I also realized I had an actual living human to converse with endlessly and to boss around, so with that, Tommy hopped in a sedan and headed off to the carpool in the sky, never to return.

A Mouse is Born

Because of Mom's medical issues, she required another surgery to get pregnant after she had me. After the surgery, when Mom didn't get pregnant for another year, she and Dad threw in the towel. They sold all the nursery furniture, looked at each other and probably said, "Well, I guess it's just us and this weird kid with the imaginary friend. We did our best."

Ladies: if you're struggling to have a second kid, just sell the nursery furniture and pregnancy will immediately follow, because that's exactly what happened to Mom and Dad. Emily Susan Underwood came into the world in 1977, completing our little family. When they brought her down the hall to Mom the very first time, Emily was crying her head off. Mom took her and put her to her breast, and she latched on right away, put her little baby fists to her cheeks, looked at Mom studiously, and started nursing like she'd been doing it for years. Mom nicknamed her "Nibbly Mouse," and the mouse part stuck, so after that, we called her Emily Mouse. My baby nickname was Pooky; neither of my parents remembers why. Fortunately for me, that nickname didn't stick because it's absolutely terrible.

Since Emily was a miracle baby, she was even more cherished than your normal second-born child. When she was about 8 months old, she got quite ill and was hospitalized for a few days, scaring my poor parents out of their minds. That year in the Christmas photos, you could see a bald spot on Em's head because they had to shave her head for her hospital IV. It's a good thing Mom was a nurse, because if I saw any of my kids with an IV in the head, they'd have to give me smelling salts to get me off the floor.

All this concern for Em just made us cuddle on her even more. Though I'm biased, Emily was one of the world's cutest babies. I was never a cuddly person, probably because as baby I was kind of thin and hideous, so I'm assuming that I didn't love the cuddles because cuddles hurt my little baby bones. Emily Mouse, on the other hand, gave my parents every bit of chubby baby cuddling a parent desires.

When Em was still a baby, Dad accepted a job as Personnel Director at the University of Texas Health Center in Tyler, Texas. Mom and Dad packed up a U-Haul, and Mom drove with baby Em strapped into a carseat in the back of our car, and I got to pile into the U-Haul with Dad for the 4 ½ hour trip to Tyler. Dad chose to spend much of this road trip grooming me to become a student at the University of Texas, teaching me all of the songs one sings at a UT football game. Either the U-Haul didn't have a radio or my Dad is just a man obsessed. It's honestly a wonder that when Mom had to pull over to breastfeed Em that Dad didn't use that time to spray paint me burnt orange. To this day, though I never attended UT, I pass for alumni at their football games, singing "The Eyes of Texas" and hooking horns with the best of them.

Once in Tyler, we moved into a modest house that was still an upgrade from our little boondocks home in Austin. One weekend, Dad took us to the French Quarter shopping center where Tyler-area car dealers had new cars on display. Dad, who considered himself a "car guy," spotted a Lincoln Continental Town Car. The price tag was $18,900. Dad told Mom to come take a look.

"This thing costs more than our first house!" Dad said.

"It should," said Mom. "It's bigger than our first house!"

When it was time for me to get out of Mom's hair (so she didn't have to listen to me singing UT football songs 24/7), she enrolled me in Caldwell Playschool, a wonderful, homey little school that smelled like someone just turned the heater on no matter what day of the year it was. Caldwell was founded by wealthy Tyler philanthropists David King (better known as "D.K.") and Lottie Caldwell. D.K. would walk the school hallways and hand out coins to baffled and delighted preschoolers. He was obviously a hit with the kids.

The Caldwells were legendary. In the 40s and early 50s in their backyard, D.K. and Lottie had their own little personal menagerie of ducks, chickens, parrots, monkeys, squirrels, and an alligator. These people had an actual alligator in their backyard in Tyler, Texas! They were kooks! Eventually, the menagerie got big enough to start an actual zoo, and in 1953, Tyler's Caldwell Zoo was founded. Today, it boasts over 3,400 animals and rivals many of the country's city zoos.

I learned a lot at Caldwell. I learned what it was like to share things, though I wasn't very good at that. I learned how to bulldoze through a line of passive kids to get one of the last remaining chocolate milk cartons sitting over ice in the cafeteria. I even had my first kiss with a boy named Danny who wore a green and yellow striped shirt. I was immediately drawn to him and I chased him relentlessly until one day I finally caught him and kissed him square on the mouth and I'm guessing nobody saw it or I would have probably been expelled on the spot. Because, even in the 70s, you weren't supposed to just go up and kiss someone without their consent, especially a preschooler.

I was an incessant talker from the start, not giving poor Emily a word in edgewise. She was a quiet, affectionate kid who was incredibly creative from the first time she could put pen to paper or arrange her toys. By the time both of us were in school, when we came home, Mom would ask us how our day went. I'd share every story, blow by blow. Afterwards, Mom would turn to Em with all that was left of her remaining energy for listening to kids talk and ask,

"How was your day, Em?"

And Em would answer, "Fine."

As Emily got a bit older, she began developing some quirky habits. In elementary school, she started saving aluminum foil from whatever things one wraps foil in, and created a small ball of foil she named Feek. Feek got kind of massive, and lived in Em's closet. I'm pretty sure I blackmailed Emily for many years, threatening to tell her secret about Feek, but now that he's taking up ample space in a landfill, the story's kind of lost its luster.

At some point, Emily got around to telling stories herself. One day when she was in preschool at Caldwell Playschool, Mom picked her up and as usual, asked how her day went, expecting the usual, "Fine." except on this day, Em said,

"You know that day?"

"What day?"

"When we went to the grocery store?"

"Uh, yeah?"

"Well we went upstairs at school, and there was hay up there, and we played, and there was a clown, and he did tricks, and a fireman came, and there was a fire truck, and.."

And Em proceeded to tell every single detail about a day that happened over two weeks ago. I'm sure Mom nearly ran off the road out of sheer amusement and awe. I'm also sure Mom was delighted that Emily had finally made the decision to share the stories of her life, and that this magic would continue. Yet sadly, I think it was another few years before Emily had a long story to tell again. We were sitting at lunch at Bruno's, one of our favorite Tyler pizza joints, when Emily began telling us about a movie she'd seen recently. She recanted the entire plot with such specificity that Mom and James and I sat dumbfounded while Emily explained each and every plot twist. Coincidentally, the movie plot she was explaining was *The Never Ending Story* so you can only imagine the family jokes that came out of that.

That same day, Em got so sidetracked regaling her story that she left her retainer on the table, and once she realized what she'd done, we had to go back to Bruno's and ask them to fish it out of the dumpster.

To this day, Em says that she gets long winded here and there because I'm so busy taking up the family airwaves that when she gets an opportunity to jump in, she makes the most of it. I can't say I blame her.

Never Sleep in Denim

When I was eight, Mom and Dad split up. As divorce experiences go for kids, it wasn't particularly traumatic for me because at an early age I recognized that my parents are very different people. Mom was a progressive thinker and my dad was more traditional; at some point it was bound to cause some problems.

Mom wanted to go back to school, finish her degree, and follow her dream of being a piano teacher. As a newly-single parent, Mom got right to business and worked several jobs to make ends meet. She taught Lamaze classes on Thursday nights at one of our local hospitals. She babysat church friends' kids at our house after school. She started teaching piano and went back to school, making straight As to nobody's surprise.

Part of Mom's divorce story includes a rather juicy Methodist church scandal. The condensed version of the story is that Mom fell in love with James, another member of the church choir bass section who was about a thousand percent more her type. They both got divorces, drove off together and got married in Santa Fe at Georgia O'Keeffe's Ghost Ranch, and we all moved into a house together and promptly became Presbyterians. Summers were lean, as Mom taught piano and money didn't come in during the summer months, and James was an advertising artist who went freelance after Brookshire's, the local family-owned grocery chain where he worked, demanded that he wear short hair, cut his beard, and wear a tie. James wasn't having any of that nonsense, so Emily and I grew up with two freelance artists with studios in our home. After school, Emily and I would figure out our own snacks while Mom taught students in the living room, and James worked on advertising art in his studio. We weren't dirt poor, we certainly weren't rich, but we were really happy.

Mom is one of the least judgmental people I know, but she does hold some strong opinions about what you should and shouldn't do. One of her biggest rules it that you should never sleep in denim. It has something to do with letting your body "air out" at night. I forgot to mention that while my mom grew up in uber-conservative Bowie, she somehow managed to become really hippie dippy later in life. And by hippie dippy, I mean that she was a hippie in most ways except she didn't smoke pot and she always wore deodorant. So when Mom told you not to sleep in denim, it wasn't about fashion. It was about letting your body breathe. To this day, I can hardly even nap wearing jeans because it feels too rebellious.

Mom wore Birkenstocks for the vast majority of my childhood, even when Birkenstocks weren't even in the least bit cool, and I certainly vocalized that point frequently. At her wedding at Ghost Ranch, she wore a beautiful American Indian-style dress. She also wore her hair in a super-short, near-buzz cut for years. We used to have poetry readings and music events at our house, and there was always a bit of a patchouli smell wafting around on those nights. Once, when I was in 4ᵗʰ grade, one of our family friend's many waiflike girlfriends had a little too much sangria and wandered into my room where I was trying to get to sleep. She sat on the edge of my bed and stroked my hair and told me she loved me until I had to conjure up Tommy to kick her out.

Mom was also quite firm on telling us that you should never lick a knife. I mean, it should go without saying, but I continue to see people do it all the time in public and I'm shocked each and every time. I think that rule actually originated when Mom and James' friend Margaret was newly divorced, and she went on a date with a man who arrived in a pale blue leisure suit and when they sat down for dinner, he licked his knife, and that was the end of that. Mom and James both had really strict rules about table manners, and for that I'm eternally grateful. If we exhibited bad table manners, James would threaten to make us sit outside and eat with the animals. I appreciate it so much now that I have kids of my own, as it will never hurt to teach your kids table manners. We aren't perfect in our family for sure, and we're all guilty of talking with our mouths full, but my sister Emily whips us into shape when she sees it because she has the best table manners of us all. She eats like a member of the royal family, but she sometimes sleeps in denim.

Mom taught us that the only time you should spit is when you're brushing our teeth. I know this is sexist, but honestly, when you think of someone spitting, don't you think of a man first? Mom's take on things is that there is nothing that forces any of us to spit so there is just no excuse for it. We don't just involuntarily spit. We choose to do it, and it's nasty. So if you spit, and especially if you make that God-awful sound beforehand, perhaps you might consider doing that business in private?

When we were little, one of Mom's most serious rules was that you should never wear a hat that belonged to someone else. To be fair, the credit for this life advice gem comes from a neighbor back when we lived in Austin when I was around four years old. The neighbors were super religious Jehovah's Witnesses, and I think Mom was so desperate for me to have friends that she looked past that weirdness so she could have a break from me here and there. Dawn was a kid who was dead serious about everything, and I'm guessing it was because she was taught that pretty much everything led to hellfire and damnation. One day I was kicking Dawn's ass at Candyland, and Dawn very seriously said, "Never wear anyone else's hat." She was so serious and Jehovah's Witness about it, I couldn't let it go, and so I passed it along to Mom. Years later we realized that she was talking about lice, and for that reason alone, I took it even more seriously and passed it along to my kids, because once you've dealt with lice, you'll do whatever's in your power to never have to deal with it again.

Mom advice wouldn't be complete without some sex advice, and lucky for Mom, Grandma Mabel pretty much nailed this one on the head. When Mom was old enough for car dates, Grandma Mabel said, "If you get in the back seat of a car, and a boy tries to put his hand between your legs, I want you to see my face." You've got to admit this is a pretty good bit of advice for a kid who might be getting frisky in the back seat of a car. It's very Pavlovian. It worked, because my mom never got pregnant as a teen, so when it came time for her to dole out advice on boys, Mom said, "If you get in the back seat of a car, and a boy tries to put his hand between your legs, I want you to see Grandma Mabel's face.'" That was a really funny bit of advice until Grandma died when I was in high school, then it got a little morbid. The great thing about this advice is that when it gets passed on to the next generation (and it already has), it becomes more and more effective and creepy because Grandma's been dead and gone for over 30 years.

Speaking of Grandma Mabel, she was the best. The part of Texas Mabel grew up in was known for its racist ideology, but she learned to evolve from that kind of thinking years beyond most of her peers. In nursing school, Mabel befriended a young black nurse named Kathy. Grandma was in her late forties, and particularly vulnerable due to being tragically widowed at an early age. Grandma and Kathy bonded through their mutual struggles in school, but also their mutual faith. They studied and prayed together in Grandma's small upstairs apartment in Denton. This bond helped Grandma tune into civil rights, and she became passionate about the issue. This was in the late 60s, just after the Civil Rights Act had passed, so Grandma thought it would be a good idea to invite Kathy to Bowie for the weekend and take her to church. When she announced this to her daughters, Mom and Aunt Pat had to persuade her not to invite Kathy, fearful that she would be placed in a potentially hurtful situation. Sadly, Bowie wasn't quite ready for an evolved Mabel High. And they certainly weren't ready for Kathy.

Grandma Mabel, pictured, top left, and her friend Kathy, seated, bottom left.

Grandma's status as an ally to women of color influenced Mom's beliefs as well. After Mom went back to work and had a job at Tyler Junior College, a man came in the copy room and began telling a story, and casually dropped the "N" word. Without hesitation, Mom said, "I find that term highly offensive and I'll thank you not to use it further." And then she walked out of the room. I like to think when she walked out, the guy just stood there open-mouthed. I also like to think that perhaps she helped him see things from a different perspective. Either way, she's a badass.

Mom passed on her open-minded, socially liberal, inclusive thinking to her children, and we're incredibly thankful for that. Now that she's in her 70s, she continues to evolve and push boundaries. In 2019, Mom, a lifelong active member of the United

Methodist Church, withdrew her membership following the vote to follow the "Traditional Plan," affirming their teachings against homosexuality.

"I went through my list of Facebook friends, and began counting how many of them are gay," she said, "And it dawned on me that if I have more than 40 gay friends, those people are more important than a church that will discriminate against them."

Mom taught us about the priceless value of international travel, of how to appreciate music from a wide variety of genres, and how to help solve big world problems by doing kind acts locally. She taught us how to make the beds with a hospital corner (though I never, ever do it that way because it's so much work). She taught us how to make s'mores. She taught us that the fork goes on the left. She taught us that when shopping for clothes, you're better off buying the shirt without writing on it, or people will say, "Here comes Amy in that same shirt again!" I have to admit that despite that advice, lately I've taken to buying some feisty feminist t-shirts, my favorite of which has Laurel Thacker Ulrich's "Well-behaved women seldom make history" quote on it, and it gets a lot of great feedback (mainly from women, imagine that!).

Most recently, Mom added a new rule to her list: Never listen to a podcast with wired headphones while cleaning the bathroom, as your phone might fall into the toilet. Just trust her. Judy knows best.

Mr. Lauderdale

From Kindergarten to third grade, I was in a carpool with my BFF Christi Cole and her older brother Doug. The Coles had one of those awesome 70s woody station wagons with an 8-track player, so every day we got to jam out to the Bee Gees, Neil Diamond and the *Grease* soundtrack to our heart's content. The station wagon was equipped with those two weird little seats that faced each other in the very back by the window. I can't remember if those seats had seatbelts, but we certainly didn't wear them, and I'm pretty sure that the far back of a woody station wagon is one of the most dangerous places for 48-pound kids to be riding, but somehow we lived to tell the tale. Anyway, that far back seat set-up provided the perfect setting for me and Christi to play countless rounds of "Hippie Hobo," a game we created that is just as terrible as you might imagine. Christi and I would hide in the floorboard until we arrived at a stoplight, at which point we would pop up and look at the person in the car behind us, only to immediately duck back down and shout out whether they were a hippie or a hobo and laugh until our little heads nearly exploded.

My mom's car offered far less exciting entertainment options.

She drove a sad brown Buick that we called The Brown Bone. The Brown Bone had a wayward pantyhose-colored headliner that began falling down lower and lower with each passing year, so much that at one point Mom referred to the inside of The Brown Bone as Mae West's bedroom.

As childhood memories go, I can't remember if there were other kids in our carpool, but if there were other kids, they must have been pretty bland characters in my life story. I do, however, remember almost every detail of a carpool drama surrounding the Andy Woods Elementary principal, Mr. Lauderdale.

First, a bit about Mr. Lauderdale. He was an elderly man (and by elderly, I'm guessing he was around 52 at the time) who was rumored to have a glass paddle for spanking kids. I never saw the glass paddle, but I absolutely believed it to be true, so even if it was just a rumor, the mere thought of it kept me in line for my entire elementary school career.

Mr. Lauderdale was a huge influence on us even though we hardly ever saw him. His office was tucked away in a far corner of the administration wing of the school, and it wasn't a place you wanted to go. At most, we would see Mr. Lauderdale on picture day and at important school functions, so this upped his status as a Scary Man of Mystery. He always wore suits, and he was bald on top. The places where he still had hair above his ears and on his neck were covered in wiry grey hair, and he had wiry grey ear hair to match. He wore big glasses that were slightly tinted, so you couldn't really tell what facial expression he was making or where he was looking.

One day, my mom couldn't pick me up and Mr. Lauderdale

took me home in his black Volkswagen Beetle. I've never gotten to the bottom of how this happened or why he offered to do this, or what happened to Doug and Christi Cole that day, but it was a big day in my collection of elementary school memories. It was the day I had one of those little kid revelations where you suddenly realized that an adult you thought was very scary was actually very sweet. He asked me loads of questions and was a great listener. Most kids didn't get the surprise luxury of a car ride with Mr. Lauderdale, so I considered myself very lucky, as if I'd just had one-on-one time with Willy Wonka or the Wizard of Oz. Because of this, I avoided asking the question that I wanted to ask more than anything;

"Do you *really* have a glass paddle? And do you really use it?"

Thirty years later, I was at a wedding reception in my home town when I spotted Mr. Lauderdale. At first, muscle memory kicked in and I was terrified all over again, but I remembered our car ride together, and how he turned out to be a sweet person, so I made a beeline to him, re-introduced myself, talked a little small talk about the bride and groom, and finally blurted out,

"I have to ask because this has been bothering me my entire life. Did you really have a glass paddle?"

He smiled from ear to ear, leaned in, and whispered,

"I'll never tell."

I think, given the creepy factor of *that* answer, we can all safely assume Mr. Lauderdale had glass paddles and then some.

Given how much we kids both admired and feared Mr. Lauderdale, it was a huge shock for us one morning when our carpool pulled up to the school and immediately, we all noticed a freshly-painted graffiti message across the otherwise pristine front of Andy Woods Elementary. Overnight, some kid or terribly drunk adult had painted "Fuck Mr. Lauderdale" in big white letters on the green panels below the windows.

Doug Cole read it out loud because he was the oldest kid and probably assumed he was the best reader since he didn't know about Mom's fruit cocktail reading program. We had no idea what it meant, but we all gasped. Until that point, I had only heard a few curse words and they all came from my father, who was pretty good at cursing but kept it PG-13 with the occasional "shit" or "damn," or when the University of Texas was losing a football game, a couple of choice GDs. All I know is that when we pulled up and Doug read the words out loud, we knew it was something really, really bad.

We got out of the car and approached the school, and because it was the 70s, nobody talked about it. We swept that business right under the rug, at least for the morning. But by the time Mom picked us up that afternoon, I could hardly contain myself. I absolutely had to know what that was all about. We piled in the car and as soon as we pulled away, I asked:

"Mom, what does 'Fuck Mr. Lauderdale' mean?"

Mom is a quick woman with a brain that runs faster than most, which came in handy during this touch-and-go parenting moment. Without skipping a beat, she said,

"Remember those two dogs we saw in the yard the other day and you asked what they were doing?," Mom asked. "Well, they were 'fucking.' 'Fuck' is a very bad word to describe sex."

Doug and Christi Cole's big brown eyes nearly popped out

of their little heads, and I wondered how long it would be before I could say that word over and over and over again, because I loved learning new words and that one was a doozie. From there, Mom turned up the soft rock on our FM radio and Christi and I launched into another rousing game of Hippie Hobo. There definitely wasn't a big discussion after that. We knew what we needed to know. One thing was for sure: that day we all learned that someone had sex with Mr. Lauderdale. We just never learned who exactly that was, or who had the guts to write about it on the front of the school for everyone to see. I like to imagine that Mr. Lauderdale eventually caught the culprit, and that they spent the next few years pulling glass shards out of their ass.

Running to Heal

Divorce stories have a funny way of having two different versions. First, you have the version from the person who hit a wall and needed to leave. Then, you have the version from the person who didn't see it coming. Realistically, the person who didn't see it coming probably saw it coming, but a troubled marriage usually also involves heaping helpings of denial.

There are two versions of divorce stories until you add kids to the mix; then it gets even messier. When Mom and Dad got divorced, Mom was the person who needed to leave, and Dad didn't see it coming. The divorce offered each of us a different version of heartbreak to experience. Mom felt a lot of guilt for causing so much pain, but she knew that in the long run, it would be a happier situation for us all. I was a fairly intuitive kid who pretty quickly picked up on how my parents' divorce was going to impact me. I was one of the first of my friends whose parents were splitting up, so I felt like an oddball at school. I didn't like feeling like an oddball, but I also knew my parents were so remarkably different that the only thing they appeared to have in common was that they had kids together. To me, it seemed like they would both be happier with other people. Also, since I was the first born, I was selfish, and I preferred peaceful moments, so if my parents weren't tense and fighting, I was happier. I also felt a need to protect my sister, who was five when all of the drama started, and pretty oblivious at that point.

The divorce was really tough on my father, a traditional family man who never thought his marriage would end. When things went south, Dad moved out and into a rather depressing apartment complex, where I imagine he spent some of the saddest, most lonely and confusing nights of his life. Years later, Dad told me that in the early months of my parents' separation, he would get off work, return to his little apartment complex, and all he could do to ease the pain was put on tennis shoes and run. It's a good thing for all of us my father isn't a drinker or a gambler. Rather, he created his own therapy with a simple pair of tennis shoes. He would run around the apartment complex until the pain was somewhat bearable, and the next day, he would repeat the process. I often think of that little scene in my head — I conjure up a short film of a man running to repair his broken heart. It's not a man running on an open trail; it's a man running around a sad apartment complex parking lot because it was safe and predictable, just like my dad.

My little film would start several years before my parents' marriage fell apart, when Dad worked as a human resources director at a hospital. My father is a handsome dark-haired man with intense brown eyes, and he speaks with marked confidence. For new hire orientation, Dad would speak in front of the new employees to welcome them to the company and talk about human resources stuff. In the little film, Dad approaches the front of the room to introduce himself when a young nurse named Pam sees my father and whispers to the woman next to her,

"He's handsome!"

The woman quickly shakes her head and whispers back, "Married. Two lovely girls. Off limits."

Pam is a good, honest woman with strawberry blonde hair and an enviable ivory complexion. When she hears the news that Dad is not an option, Pam nods her head. She's the kind of woman who doesn't want to date a married fish with two small fish at home.

The short film flashes to 1982. Mom tells Dad that the marriage is over. We see repeated scenes where Dad is running around a dreary apartment complex. There are scenes when Dad's face lights up as he pulls up to my mom's new little rental house to pick up me and my sister for his weekend. Those are the scenes where he is the happiest, but we still see the pain in his face.

In a workplace scene, Dad's secretary, a heavyset, busy bee kind of gal with a hearty laugh, walks into Dad's office, slaps a piece of paper down on his desk, and says,

"You know Pam? Pretty nurse? Second floor? This is her number. Give her a call."

Dad goes home. Maybe he runs around the apartment complex again just to help with decision-making. Maybe he microwaves a little meal, and stares at that piece of paper with the phone number on it, and his face shows us that he is completely terrified. Somehow, he gathers up enough courage to pick up the phone and dial the number, and when he hears Pam's voice, you can see him smile nervously.

When my Dad tells the story of the sound of Pam's voice when she answered the phone, his eyes are filled with such happiness I choke up every time he tells it. Dad and Pam talked on the phone for four hours every night for several nights. Then they went on their first date, and every night after that, they saw each other, and they fell effortlessly in love. When my Dad talks about those first few dates, there's innocence to that love that is magical and real. Dad describes how Pam had such a beautiful smile that it made him happy to be around her. Her smile made him smile, and his broken heart was whole again.

Dad was cautious about how to introduce us to Pam because we were so little and we'd already experienced a lot of changes in our short lives. I don't remember how he broke the news, but I remember distinctly feeling that Dad's sadness had been replaced with something pure and pleasant, and that things were turning around. My father was a few years older than Pam, and she lived at home with her mother and sister. Dad explained to us that he had met a woman, and that we were going to all go to the movies together. I'm not sure if Dad thought about that beforehand, but going to a movie was a really smart move. Introducing your little kids to your new girlfriend has to be really nerve-wracking, but at least at a movie you don't have to deal with a lot of awkward conversations together.

On the big day, Dad and Emily and I piled into the car to go pick up Pam for the movie. Dad left us in the car because you did that kind of thing back in the 80s, and walked up to meet Pam at her door. My sister Emily and I began giggling like crazy because it was all such a big mystery – who was this woman and was she going to be like? Would she be like Mom? Was she going to be tall? Short? Fat? Skinny? Blonde? Brunette? The possibilities were endless. When we spotted Dad and Pam walking down the sidewalk together, it was clear to us that Pam was The One. She was a beautiful, kind woman with glowing skin and the smile that captivated Dad.

We could tell that Pam loved us from the minute she met us. I actually think she loved us before she met us because we were Dad's girls. When I asked her about it after I had children of my own, Pam said, "You're right, but I loved you for yourselves after I met you. I've been exceedingly blessed." The feeling is more than mutual.

Always Say Yes

Some guy got really famous telling everyone that all he needed to know he learned in kindergarten, but I think that's a bunch of baloney. Most of what we need to know, we learn in the middle of puberty.

I won the puberty lottery in 5th grade, so while all of my petite girlfriends were still wearing 6x jeans, I was nearing 5'7" and getting my first period months before they showed us the puberty film. By the time we got into middle school, whenever a friend would agonize over her first period, I was a seasoned veteran ready to dole out advice. I was the Period Shaman of Hubbard Middle School. I confidently instructed wide-eyed girlfriends to wear dark pants and have their moms write a note to let the PE teacher know they had "a stomach ache" so they could sit on the sidelines and deal with cramps. I'm kind of surprised I didn't sell Midol and tampons in between classes.

I think one of life's cruelest jokes is that at the same time you're growing from a kid into a semi-adult body, society finds it necessary for you to learn how to dance in a group setting. For kids growing up in Tyler, Texas, we navigated puberty while learning how to dance in a unique East Texas phenomenon called Social Dancing.

Social Dancing was an extracurricular series of evening classes for 7th and 8th grade students designed to teach the basic concepts of boy-girl dancing, but its secondary and less obvious mission was to teach the kids some basic etiquette. It was a brilliant business plan. On Friday nights, delighted parents dropped off carloads of giggly girls in dresses and uncomfortable boys wearing jackets and ties and made a beeline across the street for stiff drinks at Bennigan's to celebrate two hours of teen-free fellowship. While the parents relaxed, the kids were left in the care of Carolyn Hardiman, a small, feisty Southern woman with big hair who deserves sainthood for devoting half of her Friday nights to doing what most of us would find impossible -- teaching oily, hunched-over teens how to dance.

Social Dancing was held in a borrowed dance studio tucked away in the corner of the Green Acres Plaza strip mall, steps away from the Merle Norman make-up studio, Figure World women's gym, a greasy bbq joint, and Green Acres Baptist Church. The entryway where the students signed in featured dark-paneled walls, big ugly trophies, and pictures of the kinds of dancers who are good enough to get trophies. The whole place smelled of dancers' feet and Ms.Hardiman's sweet perfume.

After Ms. Hardiman got us all signed in on her wooden clipboard, we clomped our Sunday shoes across the hardwood floors under the fluorescent lights and got to business. We learned partner dance classics like the box step, the waltz, and something very basic I only remember as the "forward, back, side together."

We also had many opportunities to do freestyle dancing to the fast songs, causing some of my earliest anxiety attacks. Imagine, if you will, a roomful of sweat-soaked 12 and 13-year-old kids dancing the box step to such classics as Whitney Houston's "Saving All My Love for You," then transitioning into "freestyle dancing" to Aretha Franklin's "Freeway of Love." There was some serious pre-teen jamming out going down in that studio. On Friday nights, Ms. Hardiman's dance studio became a skinny white, primarily Southern Baptist teen version of Soul Train.

The partnering of boys and girls was heavily orchestrated because Ms. Hardiman sincerely wanted to make things fair. She would divide us up, girls on one side of the room, boys on the other, and instruct the boys to go over and ask a girl to dance. But because there were always more girls than boys, some of the tall and awkward girls were forced to pair off with the other tall and awkward girls after the boys picked everyone else.

I was one of those poor ostriches. I must admit that I found some solace in the arms of those girls, not because they were great dancers, but because at least those girls didn't spend an entire Pointer Sisters ballad staring at my barely-there boobs.

Ms. Hardiman had all sorts of rules she took very seriously. The rule I remember most was her cardinal rule: Never, under any circumstances, say no when someone asks you to dance. Always say yes.

Saying yes came easy to me, as I'm a people pleaser by nature, but it was especially easy to say yes if the person asking was a boy. On Social Dancing nights I would wait, drenched in anticipatory sweat, while the short boys passed me by. Eventually one of the

48

two boys in the class who was taller than me would come over and ask me to dance. The boys were taught to extend an arm, and we would grab onto their navy blazers as they hurled us onto the dance floor. One of those boys was a tall looker who was blessed with equal parts manners and dancing skills. He helped me feel somewhat graceful as we scooted around the dance floor to the seductive strains of Patti LaBelle. But as soon as I would let my guard down and begin to enjoy myself a little, the song would change, and the other boy who was taller than me would arrive. I'd grab his elbow and spend the next 80s ballad doing everything in my power not to bump into the frightening condition that was taking place in that poor boy's pants. I never asked Ms. Hardiman if you had to say yes to the kid with the raging hard-on.

The seemingly endless Friday nights of Social Dancing culminated into a Spring Formal held at our local convention center, Harvey Hall. Thanks to PTSD, I've been able to block most of it out, but a few gut-wrenching memories from that event remain. The plan was that My BFF Christi Cole's very cool parents would take a carload of girls to Chili's after the formal. Chili's was a big deal in 1980s Tyler. We loved the low lights, the mozzarella sticks, the giant glass mugs of refillable Cokes, and the cheerful waiters who were willing to split our check 25 ways.

The night of the Spring Formal, I wore a pale blue taffeta dress with puffy sleeves. The dress was tea-length and had some tasteful lace embellishment on the torso. I felt awesome in it, and wore it with a completely unnecessary Victoria's Secret underwire bra. Because I couldn't be bothered with a purse, I shoved the

$20 my mom gave me to pay for dinner in my bra and took off for the dance.

Here, you'll note that Michael Horsley's getting a nice shot of my non-existent cleavage. Either that, or he's concentrating fully on not getting stepped on by my gigantic white shoes.

The highlight of the night was the awards portion, when Ms. Hardiman announced the winners for Best Dancer. There were several winners in the category, and I clapped and cheered as my graceful friends stepped up for their awards.

So you can imagine my surprise when Ms. Hardiman announced my name. In a blur, I walked up to accept the award, and stood frozen as friends and chaperones clapped and clapped.

Part of the honor was a feature dance with the newly awarded Best Dancers. Ms. Hardiman turned on a Motown hit, and our small group danced, showing off our sidestepping skills while the less skilled dancers watched us show them how it was done. I should have enjoyed it. But the entire time, I was completely and fully mortified, not believing for a second that my award was real.

In this photo, the pain in my face is obvious. I'm paired up with James Greer, pictured here getting down in his khakis and country club blazer, while I dance waist up, fighting back tears.

There's a reason preteen girls are drama queens. Combine all of the hormones with a tight taffeta dress and pale nude panty hose and drama is bound to take place. As the applause died down, I made a hysterical beeline to the bathroom of Harvey Hall, where I burst into sensitive, self-absorbed tears.

"This is all a big joke! They're making fun of me!" I wailed, as mildly concerned girlfriends tried to console me while looking at themselves in the mirror, puffing up their 80s bangs and reapplying blue eyeliner. "Everybody knows that I'm a TERRIBLE DANCER!"

As preteen dramas go, the tears didn't last very long. After all, a piping hot plate of mozzarella sticks was on the evening's agenda. Before I knew it, I was enjoying a late-night dinner at Chili's, somewhat convinced that I wasn't such a terrible dancer after all. I even managed to convince myself that I'd probably won the award because of my personality, or because I always said yes to every single girl and boy who asked me to dance. All in all, the night was a success, at least until the bill came, and I realized that the $20 that was supposed to be resting patiently in my non-existent cleavage had made a great escape from my Victoria's Secret underwire bra, more than likely while I was shaking my thing to the "forward, back, side together." After another dramatic bathroom scene, my BFF Christi Cole's father bailed me out and paid my share, saving the night from being a complete disaster.

I realize that the fact we were taught to "always say yes" puts a big ugly kink in the fibers of feminism that are woven in my adult being, but Tyler, Texas wasn't exactly the epicenter of feminism back then (and still isn't, for that matter). Most moms stayed at home while the dads worked. Dads were considered to be the head of the household. Everybody went to church on Sunday, as Green Acres was truly the place to be. One of the Baptist moms reminded us that we should always wear makeup to church because we "needed to look pretty for Jesus." To this day I can't get ready for a church event without thinking about looking pretty for Jesus. Because we all know that Jesus is going to shine his light a little brighter on you if you're wearing Merle Norman.

Looking back, I certainly don't think Ms. Hardiman was trying to start a 1980s "Me Too" moment by telling us to say yes. For Ms. Hardiman, it was about having the decency to dance with whomever asked you, and it's something I've taken to heart my entire adult life. I took it so seriously that in the late 2000s when I was with coworkers at The Rainbow Cattle Company in Austin and a rather stocky middle-aged woman asked me to 2-step, I said yes. I not only obliged, I didn't flinch a minute when she led me across the dance floor with her stubby fingers hooked into my belt loops. I just wish Ms. Hardiman had been there to see it.

Men are Diddlers

From the time somebody wrote "Fuck Mr. Lauderdale" on the side of Andy Woods Elementary, random sexual things started happening in my world. Maybe it's because that was when I became aware of sex, but after that, sex was everywhere. First, Doug Cole and some boys from the neighborhood found a *Playboy* magazine in a field at the end of our street, so we got to learn about pornography. Then, well before I hit puberty, Grandma Mabel gifted me with a classic manual for teens called *The Teenage Body Book*. I'm not sure why nobody told Grandma that I was too young for that much information, but once I had that thing in my hands, I became a child expert on everything from IUDs to underarm hair to syphilis. I still own it, and it's dog-eared to the page with penises because boy, those were fun to look at. I also dog-eared the pages that discussed masturbation. You know the Baader-Meinhof Phenomenon, where if you learn about something, that thing shows up all over the place?

Fast forward to the 8th grade when we took our school trip to Washington, DC. I have so many great memories from that trip, like how several of my girlfriends and I bought shirts on the mall in DC with the Heineken logo on the front that read, "Grab a Heiney." We were super classy 8th grade girls.

Our school chaperones might have told us to change shirts, except they were too busy herding kids and trying to find Kirk Hopkins, a rebellious kid who decided to abandon the group and hop on a subway by himself and go to the White House. The only problem is that he must have confused the White House with the Capitol, because that's where the rest of our giant group was located. With the chaperones dealing with our own 1980s version of a Washington DC Amber Alert, they didn't realize my girlfriends and I were wearing shirts designed to promote drinking and groping underaged girls, so that's what we wore in our school photo in front of the United States Capitol. You know all of our Methodist and Baptist parents just loved that.

At the Jefferson Memorial, we were snapping photos on cameras with real film, brushing our big Texas hair and looking at ourselves in giant locker mirrors we'd tucked into our giant drawstring purses, when we noticed a man with his penis out, diddling himself to a massive statue of Thomas Jefferson. Of course we screamed and ran and alerted the adults and authorities, but I have to admit I wasn't afraid at all; I was falling over with laughter. Finally I was seeing what *The Teenage Body Book* had explained in such graphic detail! The book simply failed to warn me that some men masturbate to public statues of Founding Fathers.

To this day when I tell people that men masturbate around me, they never believe it. Here's a handy timeline:

Berlin, December 1991. I spent a year as an exchange student in Berlin, and my mom and high school boyfriend came over to visit me for the holidays. We were on a subway in downtown Berlin, sitting down and riding along when my mom mouths to me, "That man's penis is out!" And lo and behold, a really grimy guy was sitting next to my mom with his penis out right there on a subway. That guy actually wasn't diddling, believe it or not. He was picking at fleas or crabs or whatever was crawling around down there, so we jumped out at the next stop.

Rome, June 1992. At the end of my exchange year, I traveled around Europe with three girlfriends. We were meandering through the streets of Rome when a man on a moped drove past us slowly. He made the block, then passed us again, which is when we discovered that he was driving a moped while masturbating. Italians really do talk with their hands!

I-35, around 1998. I lived in San Marcos, Texas while attending school, and worked in Austin, so I spent a lot of time on the interstate between the two places. My roommate Stephanie and I were good friends with a set of brothers who were hippie arborists who had a pretty thriving business that allowed them to follow their true passion, which was smoking pot and talking about Jesus. My car was a junker, so I often borrowed my roommate's Isuzu Trooper to drive to Austin. Those cars are impossibly high off the ground, giving me an unfortunate front row into the driver's seat of *many* a masturbating driver. I saw it ALL THE TIME. It went like this, almost every time I saw it: Man in business attire with pants yanked down, penis conveniently whipped out for view. Man is driving and masturbating. And they say men can't multitask.

I saw it so many times that people quit believing me. I would come home from work and my roommate and the arborists would ask, "How was your day?" and I'd throw down my bag and flop down on the couch and reply, "Oh, it was fine. I saw a guy jacking off again." And everyone would just roll their eyes and the brothers would get back to smoking pot.

Buda, Texas, 1999. As I was finishing school, I stopped for gas at a convenience store between Austin and San Marcos. I was filling up the car when a man walked up and said, "Hey, I think you are really pretty and I am wondering if I could drive beside you while I jack off." He might as well have been asking me for directions or to borrow a cup of sugar. I think I was actually polite about it and just said no thanks, I'd seen enough of that in my lifetime.

Or there's Jordan, the guy I met in Austin in the mid-90s while out with my friend Candace. It was one of the rare times when we spotted a guy we both thought was cute but he ended up being interested in me. We negotiated that it would be okay for me to go out with him even though Candace spotted him first. That was very kind of her, but little did she know she was doing herself a huge favor.

The guy was a looker. He had blonde curly hair and he'd hung onto the 80s preppy look and it worked. He smelled of Polo Cologne and Dunhills (in a good way). He was also very smart, and the night we met him, he was sitting alone, sipping a beer and casually reading a book. He oozed confidence and charm.

Our first date was to the movies, and I met him at one of the few "art" movie theaters we had in Austin at the time. It was our first date, and he paid for our Diet Cokes and we went into the theater to see the movie of his choice, *The Trip to Bountiful*, very possibly one of the least sexy movies in the history of film. The theater was packed with cute little white-haired moviegoers, so he led me to a seat in the very back, and I made a joke about not making out with all of those grandparents around (we had never kissed). The movie began, and while I was innocently sipping Diet Coke, Jordan reached over and grabbed my hand and guided my hand on its own personal trip to bountiful. This guy somehow managed to get horny in the first eight minutes of one of the most boring movies of all time. I guess I should have been grateful that he let me watch the trailers in peace!

Little did this poor putz know that I wasn't new to masturbating men, so my reaction wasn't the normal screaming or making a huge scene that most normal women would have made before they got hand-raped in a public movie theater. I just figured he was like most guys and just "had a need" to masturbate in public because he lacked impulse control or something ridiculous like that. But I certainly wasn't going to help out his cause, so I just pulled my hand away and said, "You're going to need to go to the bathroom and do whatever you need to do, and I am going home." So that is what happened, I guess, because I never saw him again.

Needless to say, when I see a masturbating man now, I'm rarely shocked or even afraid. I've called 311 so many times to let them know because, while I'm not particularly rattled by it anymore, I think if a kid or an old person were to see that, it might be really traumatic and possibly dangerous. What I do find so interesting is that after all these years I have never seen a woman doing it. For whatever reason, women don't seem to have a need to whip out their vaginas and diddle themselves in public.

There are always exceptions, though. I was at the airport in San Francisco with colleagues in 2015, eating a pizza and having a beer before our flight back to Austin, and I looked over at a woman sitting at another table in the same casual dining restaurant, and she was wearing a skirt that was hiked up, and lets just say she wasn't sitting in an exactly ladylike manner. Since that kind of thing is like looking at a dead raccoon on the side of the road, I kept looking until I realized she didn't have on panties. At the airport!

The only difference between this woman and the countless men I've seen diddling themselves was that she didn't diddle, so I guess she was just your average, everyday exhibitionist. But still. The last thing I want to see when I'm eating a margherita pizza is someone's vagina.

There's not much of a lesson here other than to remind you that we are all animals. Remember in the movie *Amèlie* where there's a scene that basically shows that someone is having sex at any minute of the day? Well, the same goes for masturbation. People never believe me when I tell them how many times I've witnessed a stranger masturbating, but I argue that these people just don't look around enough. Get out of your own head for a bit, and you're bound to see it. If you really pay attention to the people around you, chances are, someone will be diddling themselves, and I guarantee, that person will be a man.

Managing the Isms

At some point in my early 20s, I started having difficulty managing stress. This led to my first rounds of fairly intense panic attacks, only I had no idea what that was, so I walked around having them on a regular basis, and I just didn't tell anyone about it. Mental health issues exist in both sides of my family. Due to my Grandpa Mark's suicide (which happened before I was born), the way we handled mental health conversations in my family was just not to have conversations about mental health. I don't blame my family for this, because it was also a sign of the times. You just didn't talk about those things.

For a lot of people who struggle with stress -- and isn't that all of us at some point in our lives? -- the root of our problem is often tied to the pressure we place on ourselves. For me, it's pressure to do well at work. By "doing well," I don't mean making a pile of money, or becoming CEO of a Fortune 500 company. My definition of "doing well" professionally is that my colleagues think of me as valuable, that my customers know I'm reliable, and that nobody ever questions my work ethic.

That self-imposed pressure is terribly bad for you. My need to work hard is most definitely inherited. Mom and Dad are crazy hard workers. After they divorced, they each went off and married hard workers. Look on both sides of my family and you can't find a slacker in the bunch — those people all earned their pay in life. Take my great grandmother on my father's side, lovingly known as Great Gran. When I was a little girl, Great Gran used to lean towards me in her wheelchair and whisper, "Idle hands are the devil's plaything." There is *nothing* more effective than an ancient woman with long earlobes and chin whiskers telling you about devil's playthings to scare some work ethic into a little kid. And she practiced what she preached. Though she was in a wheelchair and no longer able to tend to a family or a farm, Great Gran quilted non-stop, keeping those wiry old hands as busy as could be.

Her words stuck with me. At a very early age, I figured that I better work hard, or the devil would start playing with my hands and I would rather just get to work, thanks. So, I got pretty good at playing the piano. Busy hands. Busy hands.

During school and college, I managed stress enough not to cause problems, but I was always known as a bit of a "stressball." When I started full-time work in my early 20s, the pressure I placed on myself began manifesting itself in the form of some ugly little anxiety attacks. I didn't know how to handle it, and that feeling fed on itself, so my anxiety worsened.

Lucky for me, when my anxiety got to the point where I felt comfortable opening up about it, my friend Candace was in grad school, getting her Master's in Social Work. I called her, and she came to my apartment with her hands full. In one hand, she held a six-pack of beer. In the other, she held a fat copy of the *Diagnostic and Statistical Manual of Mental Disorders.* I will never forget that. It's so indicative of the kind of friend she is: loyal, giving, and fully invested in helping you when you need her most. It's not surprising that Candace and I are still dear friends, and she's a successful and highly-regarded private therapist who specializes in many things, among which are anxiety disorders.

That night, with a six-pack, tears and laughter, we began searching the DSM for answers. I convinced myself that I was a psychopath, a sociopath, and a manic depressive with obsessive-compulsive tendencies. Candace was more reasonable and diagnosed me with having panic disorder. While we certainly didn't find all of the answers that night, it was a first step in identifying what was causing me to feel like I was completely out of my head. Soon enough, I began seeing a therapist, learning breathing techniques, and learning how to cope with my own definition of "normal." Candace's early intuition was spot on: I had panic disorder.

I hated the way anxiety made me feel, so I kept that secret close to my pounding chest. I was so afraid of people thinking that I was crazy. Except guess what? We're all crazy. It's just varying degrees of crazy. And guess what? Most of the normal, honest people I know have admitted that they, too, struggled with anxiety at some point in their lives. If not anxiety, then depression. If not depression, then some kind of compulsion.

My sister Emily calls these things "isms." "Isms" aren't always related to mental health. It could be that you need glasses and refuse to get them. That's your "ism." It could be that you use baby talk when you talk to your boyfriend. Well, that's not an "ism," but it is annoying, so quit it. It could be that you detest laundromats. That's your "ism." Are you getting the idea? And honestly, if you live in this day and age and don't have some kind of "ism," well, congratulations on becoming a Buddhist monk. When you get back from your silent retreat, we'll all be back here in "ism" town when you're ready to talk again.

There was a Facebook post that circulated for a while to mark Mental Health Day that had a sad little drawing of a woman in an ugly pink robe that said, "Depression, anxiety, and panic attacks are NOT a sign of weakness. They are signs of having tried to remain strong for way too long." The first time I saw it, I thought, "Of course she's depressed! That robe is terrible!"

And then I read it again, and realized that the sentiment there is meant to promote acceptance of mental health issues - and that the sentiment is a good one. But it is a tad on the dramatic side. I certainly wasn't forced to be "strong" for a long time, I just got hit square on with anxiety issues. I believe my anxiety issues have much more to do with my chemical makeup and a lot of forced pressures that I place on myself.

For those of us who struggle with our "isms," every day is Mental Health Day. Not a day goes by that I don't think about what would happen if I had an anxiety attack while driving, speaking to customers, caring for my kids, you name it. If it weren't for years off and on in therapy, an extremely supportive family, meditation and prayer, regular exercise and deep breathing techniques, I'm fairly convinced I would be trying to figure out how to leave my people and make a beeline for the nearest ashram for a long-term recovery.

And just because I can talk openly about my anxiety issues, that does not mean everyone feels that free. I really love that more and more, celebrities admit they have panic attacks or suffer from anxiety or depression. For some reason, we are comforted when a celebrity feels the same way we feel. I can't imagine that on some level, every famous person faces anxiety. If you chased me around with cameras 24/7 and followed me around in airports, I'd be a nervous wreck, too.

More and more, telling others you go to therapy isn't considered something to feel shame about, rather, it's something you can actually pat yourself on the back for doing because we all know that self-care is vital. There is absolutely no shame in having a chemical imbalance or a hormonal imbalance that makes you feel out of sorts. If you've experienced anxiety and haven't talked to someone about it, please take that step. You're worth it.

A Pole and a Parking Lot

Complex, oddball relationships are the story of my life. It started when I kissed that poor boy in pre-K, then when I hit about first grade, I moved on to loftier goals and became dead set on marrying one of the Bee Gees. I roller skated around our garage, wearing my tight peach-colored jeans with white butterfly appliqués on the pockets, singing along to "How Deep Is Your Love" in my best falsetto, dreaming of the day I would become Mrs. Gibb. I later set my sights on John Travolta, and imagined that he would wear the same thing he wore in *Saturday Night Fever* to our disco-themed wedding. At some point, I dumped John Travolta for Shaun Cassidy.

As I got older, I never really knew what my "type" was. My mother always gently suggested that I marry a doctor or a mechanic – not because of the supposed financial stability such jobs offer – but because I'm a hypochondriac and for years I drove cars that needed a lot of attention. I tried taking her advice. I dated a cardiologist for about ten minutes. Setting up our first date took ages because he was always on call, and when we finally got together, he told me point blank he was looking for a quiet woman who would be a good mother. I knew I wanted kids eventually, but in looking for a "quiet woman," he was fully admitting he wasn't interested in a woman with an opinion. Since I have at least a million of those, that wasn't going to work. For a short time, I dated a man who conveniently forgot to tell me he was a single father. He kept his dating life and his fatherhood life in separate buckets, so at the same time he told me was falling in love with me, he decided to share the bonus news that he had a toddler. However, his house offered zero evidence that he had a child. That relationship ended abruptly for obvious reasons. After that, I dated a guy that I will forever refer to as Rat Boy. That relationship lasted far too long. It ended with my friend Candace yelling something at him from the top of our apartment staircase that scared Rat Boy enough to take his bad tattoos and nipple ring and scurry back to his waterbed, never to be seen again.

My inability to find the right kind of man mirrored my inability to find the right kind of life's calling. I changed majors constantly, moving from music to international relations to my most fitting major, undecided. My sweet mom was funding this life experiment, so I decided it was time to give her a break and figure out what I wanted. I did some temp work. I waited tables and figured out pretty quickly that I wanted more out of life than rolling silverware and breaking my back trying to carry trays full of food. I moved around and ended up in Austin, where I took a job at a hotel, and worked my way up from telephone operator to front desk to concierge. By this time I was approaching my mid-20s, drifting around unsure of what was going to happen next.

Late one Sunday afternoon, fate and a stroke of unfortunate choices helped me decide what was going to happen next.

That morning, I decided to treat myself to a movie, and since I couldn't find anyone to come along, I decided to go it alone. At that point in my life, the thought of going to a movie alone was unheard of – it would be like wearing a neon suit that screamed, "Single. Alone. Sad Sack. " However, because I was single, alone, and going through a bit of a sad sack period, I figured I might as well make the most of it. I decided to go see the Christian Slater movie, *Bed of Roses*. That decision pretty much sums up the state of my life in 1996.

It was a gorgeous day. The sun was at that beautiful place just before it sets where it casts a golden blanket of light over the city. I stopped at the drive-thru at Long John Silver's and grabbed a sweet tea and wedged it between my legs for the ride. I rolled the windows down to smell the fresh air. Creedence Clearwater Revival's "Proud Mary" played on the radio. As I sang along, I popped the visor down to block the sun from my face, and took my hands off the steering wheel so I could roll my fists in circles and sing.

"Rollin'! Rollin'! Rollin' on the river!"

This scenario is pretty much a perfect example of what not to do while driving, quite possibly equally as dangerous as having four back-to-back Jagermeister shots before getting behind the wheel. The combination of sweet tea between the legs, CCR, late-day sunshine and driving while dancing? Let's just say I didn't make it to the movies that day.

As I sped through the shopping center parking lot, I didn't see the concrete base at the bottom of a huge large pole where a retail sign used to be. I was probably going a good 30 miles an hour when my gray Honda Accord met its demise.

Meanwhile, a family in a Suburban sat in a fast food drive-thru located in the same shopping center parking lot. While they waited on fried chicken and mashed potatoes, the father saw the entire thing take place. He jumped out of his car and told his wife to call 911 as he ran across the parking lot to save me. Smoke rose from the hood. The father was still running toward me when he saw me get out of the car, stand there for a second, then promptly and calmly lay down on the ground beside the smoking car.

My recollection is a little fuzzy, but I remember the sound and the feeling of the initial impact, and then feeling my left foot snap like a dry twig. When my head popped up after the impact, I knew my foot was broken. Somehow, I had enough wits about me to get out of the car, which I figured was about to catch on fire because of all of the smoke. When I opened the door and stood up for a second, I was dizzy and out of it. All I knew to do was to lie flat down on the ground and wait for help.

From there, I mainly remember sounds. I heard Father Hero Man running across the pavement, my car hissing in misery, and sirens. Within minutes I was surrounded by multiple fire trucks, police cars and ambulances. The attention was kind of over-whelming, but I loved it. Many witnesses gathered around, and I could hear them commenting on how, no, there wasn't another car in the accident. The car just drove straight into the concrete base. Bam. If I weren't in shock and shivering uncontrollably, I would have laughed. What a ridiculous thing to witness. Car drives through parking lot. Car slams into pole without slowing down. Pole 1, Car 0.

The EMT who was assessing me asked me a hundred questions. Even in my sad state, I could recognize that he was quite a looker, and thought about asking if he had plans to see *Bed of Roses* any time soon. I smiled up at him as he leaned into his walkie-talkie thingy and said,

"The victim appears to have urinated from the impact."

Had I not been soaking up the attention, I might have opted to die right there.

"I did NOT urinate!" I wailed, "That was sweet tea from Long John Silver's!" That made me look like less of a loser, I'm sure. Father Hero Man started to laugh.

"Now, I'm going to need you to squeeze my leg," the EMT said, squatting beside me.

I reached up to squeeze. I was fine. I squeezed hard.

"Whoa, there!" he groaned, as I realized I'd squeezed him in a rather sensitive spot. And when I say sensitive spot, I mean penis.

That's about the time I passed out, probably from embarrassment. I honestly don't remember much after that. To this day, I don't even know if I rode in the ambulance or if my friend came and picked me up, because Father Hero Man called people for me. The next thing I remember was being at my friend's mother's house, recovering, and several days later, Dad and Pam came to pick me up to take me to my home town to continue my recovery.

I had a broken foot, a badly bruised torso, and an even more badly bruised ego. To this day when I tell the story of hitting a pole in a parking lot, people shake their heads and laugh. To this day, if "Proud Mary" comes on, I change the station immediately or leave the room. It doesn't matter if it's the Tina Turner version or a Muzak version in the grocery. "Proud Mary" is my bad luck song, and CCR is my bad luck band.

The broken foot made it impossible for me to continue working as a hotel concierge, and my insurance was so crappy that I didn't have disability coverage, so I was forced to quit my job. Thanks to a network of friends, a hotel coworker hooked me up with his friend who worked at an answering service. Soon, I had a job as a medical answering service telephone operator, where working on crutches is fine because you're sitting all day anyway.

The fateful CCR/pole in a parking lot incident was a screaming reminder that I was single, without a degree, and suddenly temporarily disabled. I vowed to get back to school as soon as I could walk again, and this time I knew what I wanted to do. I wanted to write. I got my cast off, signed up for classes during the day, changed my major to journalism, and answered medical answering service calls at night.

And then I met Tim.

Girlfriend on a Napkin

If you had told me when I first met Tim Arndt that we would end up together, much less married, I would have laughed in your face for about an hour. Tim Arndt worked at the medical answering service in the sales department. When a physician bought a pager from Tim and needed us to take their after-hours calls, my department handled that.

I should probably stop and clarify what a pager is for those of you under 40. A pager was, at the time, the only way you could reach your doctor after hours unless you had a carrier pigeon or the Ricola guy to yell your messages at you from a nearby mountaintop. A pager wouldn't let you do really anything except send a weird numeric text message, and it worked one way. The little box on your hip would vibrate, you'd see a number, and you would call the person back from a landline. Please don't make me explain landlines.

As pagers became more sophisticated through the years, you could send alphanumeric pages, but again, the person with the pager could only run over to a real telephone to call you back. Can you even imagine how inefficient this could be for a heart surgeon? Considering the lack of sophistication in this industry at the time, it helps explain why I got yelled at by doctors on a regular basis.

Tim was not on my radar in the least where romance was concerned. For starters, he was married with two children, and more than a decade older than me. Also, I've never believed in fishing off of the company pier, and just like my stepmother Pam, I knew that dating a married fish with two fish at home absolutely wasn't for me.

Tim is a super likeable guy. He's a tall, loud people person with a huge laugh. He can quickly talk your arm off and be halfway through your second one as you try to break away, but because he is so positive and fun, you can't help but stick around. Back then, I was probably one of the only people who groaned when Tim showed up. I thought he was a nice enough guy, but because my role was to juggle answering calls and entering new doctors in our system and setting up their pagers, when Tim came bounding down the stairs to the basement where our office was located, I wasn't exactly thrilled. Tim's presence meant more work for me.

Another reason Tim and I were such an unlikely and impossible match was that Tim was so metrosexual I wasn't quite sure he was heterosexual. His wardrobe didn't point to a straight man's taste. For starters, he owned a mustard yellow suit. My coworkers who knew I worked closely with Tim on pager orders would come up to my desk and say, "Tell Tim Arndt to wear his mustard yellow suit!" And we would laugh our heads off about it because who owns a mustard yellow suit (and a linen one at that!)? Because Tim was always meeting with doctors, he was impeccably ironed and dressed to the nines. Pair that with his loud laugh and his tendency to overuse the word "cute," and I just couldn't fathom how a man that flamboyant could possibly be straight.

The surefire indicator that Tim was gay was when we had a rare ice storm in Austin and a group of us had to spend the night to answer medical emergency calls. Tim braved the ice and drove over to bring a tray of sandwiches he had made at home. I don't know many straight men —correction: I don't know ANY straight men — who voluntarily make sandwich trays. He also brought a movie for us to watch in between calls, and of all movies to select, he picked *The Bird Cage*.

Are you picking up what I'm laying down? Tim Arndt was SO gay!

Except he wasn't. Our story is complicated, as things like that go. I didn't know much about Tim's personal life, but I'd heard rumors that his marriage was on rocky ground. Meanwhile, I was working while finishing up college, and eventually quit the medical answering service to force myself out of the literal and figurative basement where I worked for several years. Around the time I quit my job there, Tim went through an ugly, painful divorce. Before that divorce happened, Tim expressed interest in me in a way that convinced me he wasn't gay. Never mind that Tim was off limits, I didn't think dating a man Tim's age was the smartest idea for me, so I tried dating guys my own age, and a few who were quite a bit younger.

Tim eventually moved into a tiny home in the neighborhood where his kids lived. Despite a long period of not speaking, soon after Tim moved into the small house, he called me and invited me over, and that was that — I fell in love with my boisterous, almost gay former co-worker. It was so unlikely, in fact, that the only thing that could have possibly foreshadowed our relationship was that Tim and Shaun Cassidy were born just a year apart. Otherwise, everything about our relationship pointed to potential disaster.

We dated for a while before introducing each other to the other important people in our lives, especially his children. Looking back, I know we were both afraid that if we opened up our relationship to others, it might not work. When the time was right, I called Mom to give her the news.

"I've fallen in love," I said.

"Tell me about him!" Mom said, enthusiastically.

"His name is Tim. We worked together at my last job. He recently went through a divorce. He has two kids. He smokes. He's Catholic. His laugh sounds like a cross between a machine gun and Bert from *Sesame Street*. He's 14 years older than me. And he just quit his job."

I waited for a moment as she let that sink in.

"Does he have his arms and legs?" Mom asked.

"Well, yes…" I answered, perplexed.

"At least he has that going for him!" Mom said. "I'm sure he's perfect."

This is not a typical response for most, but this is my mom we're talking about. She has the unique ability to trust her kids to make the right choices. I know few parents who are able to do this. I'm not even that kind of parent! It's as if Mom was born without the judgment gene, and it's been a relief to have that kind of mom, considering how many mistakes I've made in my life.

A short time after I told Mom about Tim, she drove down to Austin to meet him. Mom and I found a table outside at Flipnotics, my favorite coffee shop (may it rest in peace eternal). When Tim walked across the parking lot and Mom saw the look in my eyes when my eyes met Tim's, she smiled and said,

"Oh, Amy. He's The One."

She was right. The person who has known me the longest knew that Tim and I shared something unique and that despite the countless challenges ahead of us, there was no denying our deep connection. However, not everyone in my life was that flawlessly supportive. Many people pushed back, and they had a right to do so. On paper, the whole deal looked like a recipe for endless drama and heartache.

Eventually, Tim and I decided it was time for me to formally meet his kids. How my Dad handled introducing us to Pam, paired with Tim's ability to put his kids' feelings first, helped inform the timing of our meeting. And though I'd been through the scenario myself as a kid, it certainly didn't prevent me from being incredibly nervous.

Tim's parenting philosophy has always been, "Parenting is a series of bribes and distractions." If Tim Arndt is good at one thing, it's knowing how to set the stage for a positive experience, and how to offer up a beautiful distraction. McDonald's, for kids in Austin in the late 90s, was the perfect distraction. Terrible food, terribly bad for you, I know, I know, but hello, Playscape! And soft serve! And those creepy but delicious McDonaldland character cookies! At this time, Matthew was 5 and Stephanie was 4, and Matthew's biggest source of self confidence was that he was already riding his bike without training wheels. Tim orchestrated a bike ride from their little house to McDonald's, and the scene was set so that I would happen to be there and bump into them. I loved this plan, because it gave me an easy escape route. If things weren't working out, I had my own car there and I could bail.

The first part of our meeting is a complete blur, except I do remember wearing a red ribbed hoodie sweater and some ugly khaki pants, so the kids probably thought I was meeting them after getting off work from my job at Target. I sat at the table with Stephanie while Tim ordered, and we waited in silence while she eyed me suspiciously with her big brown eyes. Matthew was the shy one, and stayed close to Tim, then ran off to the playscape to escape the awkwardness.

I love kids. I babysat in high school, and always had good rapport with the little ones. Lucky for me, my first meeting with Matthew and Stephanie went very well overall. I was not introduced as a girlfriend. I was a friend of Tim's, but even then I'm pretty sure the kids were onto us.

At some point during the meeting, we began drawing pictures on napkins. I'm guessing I initiated this to calm my nerves, but also because my stepfather James was always drawing on things and it was fun to be that person.

Stephanie drew a picture of Tim and Matthew and Stephanie on bikes, and added me to the picture. I saved that napkin for years until it finally disintegrated. I was the girlfriend on a napkin, and while it was just a simple drawing, it was big. In some small way, that drawing meant I had passed the first test.

Whatever the Case May Be

For most of the early days when Tim and I were dating, I maneuvered through the process like a teenage boy with greasy popcorn hands trying to get to second base in a crowded movie theater. Let's just say it was a pretty awkward time. I handled the situation by setting expectations early: I was not applying to be a substitute mother. My goal was to make it clear to the kids that they had, and would always have, a mother and a father who loved them, and I was simply an extra adult that would be there to support and protect them if they needed it, and love them when the time felt right.

Matthew, who was 5 when I entered the scene, was the easier of the two kids. I say this very openly because both of my stepkids know it's a true statement. Matthew was a "typical" first born. It was obvious he felt a crushing responsibility to care for Stephanie, who was just a little over a year younger than Matthew. Despite his fierce protection of his sister and his loyalty to his mother, Matthew's sensitive little soul found the grace to accept me.

I decided to focus on spending quality time with Matthew because he was willing to let me hang out with him. Tim and Matthew loved cars and fixing things, and one day they found one of those little kid-sized pink Barbie cars on the side of the road that someone had thrown away, so of course they took it home and promptly souped it up. They stripped off the pink paint and painted it red, and swapped its wimpy battery for one much more powerful. Matthew loved to drive the car around and around the front yard and down the sidewalk, especially because the car had a pretty key flaw in that it didn't have functioning brakes, so when it came to the point where the car was about to crash into a tree, Matthew would jump out and roll around on the ground and laugh until he was wiped out. He would mimic an announcer's voice and ride around the track, yelling,

"And he's off! Matthew Arndt in car #17, taking the turn at a crazy speed! He's winning! He's going to make it! And he is jumping out of the car as it crashes!"

I would sit on the front porch watching him and laughing, and one afternoon, I got so into watching his show that I stood by the tree where he was driving and when it came time for him to crash into the tree, he miscalculated a bit and crashed into me, and we both fell on the ground, each in some level of pain. Tim came running out to see about us, and he made a beeline for Matthew, who was crying and shaken.

As I waited for Tim to turn his attention to my minor injuries, I realized that no matter what, Tim's kids would come first, and as much as that was a little hard for me to accept (because at that very moment I also had an "owie" that needed attention), it made me love him more. That's how it should be. The kids should always come first.

Matthew and I continued to bond through physical activity,

which I really recommend to people dating someone with little kids. I went to a used sport store and bought professional boxing gloves for both of us, and willingly let him beat the crap out of me in the front yard. I figured that he could take out some of his frustration and anger about his parents' divorce out on my flabby stomach.

While things worked pretty well when it came to bonding with Matthew, my early relationship with Stephanie was a totally different story. When I came onto the scene, Stephanie was in preschool, and she wasn't up for a new woman in her life. For starters, she was confused about her parents' situation, and, like all other normal kids, wanted her parents to get back together. I was confused as well. When I was around Stephanie, she would usually greet me with a dark-eyed scowl. Other times, she would invite me to play Barbies, or ask me to serve her ice cream. Because her reactions to me were all over the place, I was always slightly on edge when Stephanie was around. I worried that we would never connect. I considered that she might smother me in my sleep. I began having nightmares that she was chasing me with a butcher's knife with ice cream dripping off of it.

When Stephanie was in first grade, she became a Girl Scout Daisy. One weekend when the kids were at Tim's, the Girl Scout troop meeting was a nature hike at a local park. Tim, always encouraging my relationship with the kids, suggested that I take Stephanie. At the time, I would have rather eaten live earthworms. I had never attended a Girl Scout meeting in my life, and wasn't sure I wanted to start by going with a kid who barely tolerated my presence, but I decided to accept the challenge.

Tim, sensing that my losing my Girl Scout meeting virginity would leave me in no shape to drive, decided to drop us off at the park. As he drove off, I considered running full force in the direction of the car, throwing my shoes at the back windshield in a wild effort to get his attention like that dramatic scene in *Hope Floats* where Birdie's dad leaves her in the dirt as he drives away. Instead, I held back my natural inclination to panic, and followed a much more confident Stephanie to the space where the mothers and daughters were gathering. I quickly assessed the scene. The warm and friendly troop leader was absent, leaving another, somewhat sullen parent volunteer in charge. Another parent I knew from work, who was my go-to person for conversation, was also not there. This left me with a group of women that I didn't know at all, so I stood on the outskirts of the group, picking at my nail polish as Stephanie and the other Daisies frolicked around.

The sullen mother who volunteered to lead the meeting gathered the group together. I could tell right away she meant business. She stood with confidence and held three fingers up in the air. Immediately, the wild first grade mayhem stopped. The girls all stood at attention, holding three fingers in the air, facing their temporary leader. I'd been there less than half an hour and they were already busting out secret hand symbols?

"Now, girls," the mother said to the group of hypnotized Daisies, "This is a very, very dangerous trail. There are steep areas where you can fall and get hurt."

The girls, transfixed at the thought of plunging to their deaths in Daisy vests, hung on to her every word. I resisted the urge to roll my eyes and groan, knowing that this park's tallest peak was a smidge over three feet tall. I decided to stay positive, imagining in my play-pretend mind that after the hike, the sullen substitute troop leader would award me with a hiking pin to attach to my imaginary adult-sized Daisy vest.

"Because we want you to be safe, I need you to listen to the rules," the mother said. "Please get in line in groups of two. We're going to use the Buddy System. Each girl needs to stand by their mommy."

She paused, looked at Stephanie, looked at me and frowned, unsure of what to say. She looked up into the air, mentally scanning the Girl Scout Leader guidebook for how to appropriately address non-mommy types.

"Or....." she said, carefully, waving her hand in a grand, dismissive gesture, "The girlfriend of your father, whatever the case may be."

And with that, she began nervously shuffling girls and mommies or whatever the case may be into a two-by-two line. Without the luxury of a getaway car, I stood there, fighting back the desire to burst out laughing and sob with embarrassment all at the same time. Several of the more compassionate mothers smiled at me and shrugged. Some just grabbed their girls and got in line.

Stephanie handled it like a pro. I honestly think she felt sorry for me because kids are awesome like that. She grabbed my hand and led me to the line like nothing ever happened. We started our hike, did some obligatory leaf rubbings, and returned with zero broken bones and one mildly bruised ego (mine). I had a couple of conversations with the compassionate mothers. All in all, we had a pretty nice time.

It's really funny that the woman who made me feel so uncomfortable ended up living right around the corner from us, and while I totally know her name, I always refer to her as "Whatever the Case May Be." To this day, she is still weird around me. I should probably have thanked her. She helped me learn that when you're dating someone with kids, it's not always comfortable, and you don't always feel welcome.

One of these days when I get my adult-sized Daisy vest, I'll have lots of pins. I'll get a Naive Cookie Mom pin. I'll have one for Patience, and it will be an image of the hours I spent with a panicked homesick and misfit child at the Girl Scout sleepover. I'll be holding out a dark chocolate bar, convincing her that sleeping on an air mattress in a musty cabin was actually worth it. But the pin I'll put in the most prominent position will be for sticking with it despite my insecurities of dating a man with children. That one will be the "Whatever the Case May Be" pin, and it will be a rendering of me, but instead of holding up three Girl Scout fingers, I think I'll just point my middle finger proudly in the air.

On the Fence About Weddings

I'm sorry to admit this, but when it comes to weddings, I'm not sure where I stand. There's a lot about weddings I hate. I realize this is one step away from saying I hate puppies or Christmas. I just don't like the drama associated with weddings, and they all seem to be jam-packed with drama from the moment the couple gets engaged. Of course, I like the actual moment where the bride and groom get married, and I do love a good reception. For a few years, my sister and I were getting a little Hilton-sister famous for how much fun we could be at receptions. That probably has something to do with getting busted by security for dancing in a fountain at our friend Caitlin's wedding.

We all have our wedding disaster stories. The first one I witnessed was when my cousin Kassie got married. I was a little girl, and Kassie was my older girl cousin that I worshiped, so I had a blast because she asked me to pass out the little bags of rice to toss at the end of the wedding. (That was back when people pelted rice at newlyweds.)

This side of my family lived in the country, and the wedding was held in the local Methodist church. For the most part, it was a lovely wedding. Lovely, that is, until Grandma Mabel — a bit of an attention seeker — showed up tanked on margaritas and made a few embarrassing scenes and had to be hushed. The ceremony itself went off without a hitch, and as we were leaving the sanctuary after the wedding, my great Aunt Ramey Gene, a complete Southern belle, said (quietly at first),

"The church is on fire. The church is on fire. THE CHURCH IS ON FIRE!"

And lo and behold, someone had knocked over one of the candelabras at the front of the church, and the church was indeed on fire. In just a matter of seconds, that place smelled like burning Methodist sanctuary shag carpet mixed with tall vanilla pillar candles. A savvy usher found a fire extinguisher, saving the day and the church.

Although I'm not a huge fan of traditional weddings, I really love a destination wedding. A lot of people think destination weddings are selfish, and I understand why, but really, it's a brilliant way to weed out a ton of people, which weeds out a ton of stress. Generally speaking, the cream rises to the top and you get the people willing to shell out a few grand to take a gigantic field trip with other fun adults. The best kind of destination wedding is the one where you spend the majority of the time bellied up to an all-inclusive swim-up bar where there's enough chlorine to kill off the adult pee that everyone is sitting in because have you counted how many people actually get out of the pool to go to the bathroom at adult swim-up bars? At these magical adult pee swim-up bars, the bartenders serve you bottomless booze and call you "Preciosa." That kind of destination wedding also offers chilaquiles, hot dogs, and french fries pretty much non-stop, helping soak up the booze you consumed all day at the swim-up bar. How can you not love that?

My friend Joanne got married in Mexico at an all-inclusive resort, and I was one of the bridesmaids, along with my other two great friends, Amy and Amy. (Yep, if you're counting, that's three Amys and a Joanne). The wedding was an absolute blast, and relatively drama-free. Since the bridesmaids got along so well, we agreed to divvy up the toast at the wedding. Up until that wedding, I took great pride in my wedding toasts. I did one at my dearest friend Candace's wedding when I was the maid of honor, and it got loads of laughs and very well may be the reason that I got interested in doing stand-up comedy years later. There was something very satisfying about the little old relatives telling me what a great job I did. After trying out stand up comedy, I have to say that little old relatives make a much nicer audience than single 24-year-old male hipsters, which is why if I try stand-up again, I'm doing it at a nursing home.

I believe a successful wedding toast needs to include a few things to laugh about as well as something sentimental. That way, you get the best of everyone's emotions while they are having big feelings about the wedding couple. That was absolutely the plan with Joanne and Chris' toast. I planned ahead. I scribbled down my outline on a piece of paper in case I got lost. The goal was to give a short and sweet toast and pass the mic onto the next bridesmaid.

I have no clue what happened, but I completely bombed.

Just thinking about it after all these years makes me cringe. For starters, my goal was to talk about how they'd been together for so many years and that it was just a matter of time before they got married because they were absolutely meant to be. I was going to tell the story of how Joanne came to work to show me her ring after Chris proposed, but because the ring was too big so she didn't have it on her ring finger, I didn't know if I should congratulate her or tell her I was sorry that he gave her a middle finger ring.

It should have been funny, but my delivery was terrible and it ended up making it look like Chris messed up by not knowing her ring size in advance, and it also kind of poked fun at the fact that it took Chris so long to ask Joanne to marry him. It was awful. Let's just say the little old relatives didn't exactly approach me afterwards to tell me how great of a job I'd done, and thank goodness the two other bridesmaids bailed me out and did a great job themselves or it would have been a complete disaster. I'm so thankful that it wasn't videotaped, and even more thankful that the next day, we all got back to the swim-up bar and nobody talked about it again.

Several years ago, my friend Ursula had a crazy extravagant wedding and I was one of the bridesmaids. Ursula's family is from the Philippines, and she shipped down countless cousins and good family friends she's known her whole life that she hilariously refers to as "fake cousins." To get all of the Filipinas from A to B, Ursula had to rent huge tour buses to schlep them from their downtown hotel to the venue, which was in the middle of nowhere. All in all, it was a really fun wedding and you wouldn't have believed how fancy the reception was. They had countless food stations, open bars, an old-timey photo booth, and even an ice cream station. It was basically like a pop-up mini-Disneyland.

Before the wedding, we were getting ready in the bridal suite, which was in the beautiful main house on the property. On top of the usual pre-wedding jitters, it was also a really emotional day because Ursula's mom had passed away several years back from breast cancer, and of course there was a big void there that everyone tried to replace by loving up on sweet Ursula all day long.

Some smart cookie brought in food for the bridal suite, since we were sipping champagne a little faster than the recommended pre-wedding cocktail hour. While the other bridesmaids were circled around Ursula admiring her hair and makeup, I made a beeline for the cheese plate and began shoveling in cheese. (I eat when nervous. And excited. And sad. You get me.)

I was a little emotional watching my friend get ready on her wedding day. I was also a little exhausted, and a tad tipsy. It was one of those times where you're soaking in the energy of the situation, and I watched everyone hustling and bustling around and felt truly present. At one point, I forced the wedding photographer to take a picture of me sitting in a chair so I could capture the essence of the moment, only when the photos came back, we all laughed until we cried because I ended up looking like I was posing for an advertisement for one of those law firms that represents car wreck victims and gets their client one hundred forty seven thousand, eight hundred sixty eight dollars and twenty four cents.

I was so in the moment that after my little photo session, I went back to work on the cheese plate and while reflecting on the moment, inhaled a piece of cheese with cheesecloth still on it, and in the next moment, I began to choke.

For a woman who's had a lifetime of paranoia about choking, for some reason, it didn't go down like you see in the movies. I didn't wave my arms back and forth and display the International Sign of Choking. I didn't ram my stomach against a nearby chair or pointy counter. Rather, I just had a realization that instead of air in my air hole, there was a wad of cheesecloth. I thought of having someone call 9-1-1, but then I realized that by the time an ambulance made its way out to the middle of BFE, I'd be a dead bridesmaid on my friend's wedding day.

It was immediately evident to me that I was going to have to save myself. Nobody had a clue what was going on because brides take up all of the attention, so I rather calmly put my drink down and reached into my throat and began yanking cheesecloth out of my throat like a magician pulling out a string of tied-together colored scarves. By the time anyone figured out what was happening, I had already saved my own life. My only disappointment was that the wedding photographer didn't capture it on camera because that would have been really fantastic. The good thing about the choking incident is that in all of the photos, we're laughing really hard about the fact that I nearly croaked on Ursula's wedding day.

I am glad I didn't die on Ursula's wedding day, because that would have really put a damper on things, and I don't think they would have gotten deposits back so they would probably have had to carry on without me, and that's really funny to me. Then again, I have a very odd sense of humor, and I've laughed when I've heard more than one story of someone actually dying at a wedding. My favorite is the man who dropped dead while dancing the Macarena at a wedding. I know it's not funny, but then again, it IS. It brings up so many questions! Can you imagine that happening at your wedding? Isn't that a pretty big sign that the wedding is cursed? And then what happens? Do people just bag up Uncle Jerry and proceed to cut the cake and blow bubbles as the couple leaves for their honeymoon? Or is the honeymoon cancelled because Uncle Jerry had to take all the attention and have a funeral?

I don't recommend dying at someone's wedding. It's kind of rude, really. But if you're going to do it, rather than choking on a string of cheesecloth or catching on fire, you might as well go out dancing.

Why Don't They Sell Unplanned Pregnancy Birth Announcements?

By the time I was nearing 30, it wasn't clear if Tim would ever bite the bullet and marry again. In his defense, he didn't exactly have a great taste in his mouth where marriage was concerned, and I think he feared that if we were to marry, we would slip into the same patterns that caused the downward spiral of his first marriage. Understandable, for sure. However, this didn't mean I didn't want marriage and kids myself. It was a tough place to be because I didn't want to give Tim an ultimatum, because those are terribly manipulative. So I decided to just be *mildly* manipulative.

"I know you may not want to get married again," I'd say, "But if it's not in the cards for us by the time I turn 30, I may need to move on."

Once I began to realize that Tim and I might not be on the same page, I started making plans to actually move on. Because I was deeply embedded in Matthew and Stephanie's life, this wasn't easy. The mere notion of leaving was heartbreaking; the mere thought of staying made me worry that I might spend my 30s unfulfilled.

Career-wise, I wanted to write in some capacity and actually get paid for it. I began making serious plans to move to New York. At the same time, I applied for a writing job in Dallas at their LGBT publication, *The Dallas Voice*. I drove to Dallas for the interview, and the editor asked the obvious question,

"Why should we hire a heterosexual woman to write for an LGBT magazine?"

It was a fair question. Lucky for me, when I put my heart to it, I can be rather charming. It's an East Texas trait. I explained that while I wasn't gay myself, I was a hugely supportive ally, but more than anything, I was a good writer, and I would do a good job. He wouldn't regret hiring me.

A few weeks later, I went out for margaritas with my best gal pal Candace to talk to her about my thoughts about possibly moving to New York, or even to Dallas if I got the job at *The Dallas Voice*. During dinner, I started feeling strange. I went into the bathroom, washed my hands and looked at myself in the mirror and asked the woman looking back at me,

"Are you pregnant?"

I went back to the table and told Candace.

"Oh, I'm sure it's just nerves," Candace said, reassuringly. She's very good about reassuring people.

Several days later, I wasn't feeling better. I was nauseous and exhausted. I did the math, and it was beginning to be obvious that Aunt Flow was skipping her visit. Tim went out to buy a pregnancy test, and two drops later, the test came back positive.

I was completely freaked out. What about moving to New York? What about Matthew and Stephanie? What about Dallas? What about Tim? What would my parents think?

"What are we going to do?" I asked, desperate and hysterical.

"We're going to get married and have this baby."

And that was that.

Tim Arndt loves to tell people that he trapped me, just like the cliché of the high school cheerleader who traps the quarterback. Except it's all in reverse, and that works for me. Tim tells everyone that he didn't want me to leave him, so he purposefully knocked me up to keep me here. While we didn't sit down and plan on getting pregnant, it was our story and it was meant to be.

A few weeks later, as we started to figure out how to make life in a two-bedroom house work with two kids and a newborn, I received a call from the editor at the *The Dallas Voice*.

"Congratulations, the job is yours," the editor said. He told me I'd be covering city council meetings and stories on local government.

"I am so honored," I said. "Thank you."

I actually didn't say anything near as eloquent. I can't remember what in the world I said, but knowing me, I probably rambled on with a hundred thank yous and I'm sorrys, but I finally just said what had to be said.

"While I am so flattered by the offer, I have news for you that I doubt you've heard from a candidate before. I'm pregnant. It's totally unexpected."

"You are correct," he said. "I've never had that one before."

He wished me the best, and while part of me wondered what

it would have been like covering city council meetings for an LGBT magazine, it didn't matter. I was making the right choice, and there was no turning back.

We told people in waves, and most everyone was extremely supportive and not at all judgmental. At one point during the family phone calls, one of my relatives expressed grave concern that I was marrying a Catholic, and how I should be loyal to my Methodist roots. I wanted to tell her to be thankful I wasn't becoming Wiccan, but I just let it be.

I learned quickly that when you get pregnant unexpectedly, they don't really make birth announcements for that. I think it would be terrific if they did. Like a sarcastic photo of two people peering at a pregnancy test and the card reads, "Oops!" Or, a card that simply reads:

> *First comes love*
> *Then comes positive pregnancy test*
> *Then comes wedding*
> *Then comes baby!*
> *We're unconventional and we love that!*

Unfortunately, at the time I didn't have as much of a sense of humor about it all because I was in such a state of shock. Maybe I'll start an unplanned pregnancy and shotgun wedding series of cards. I think they would be a big hit.

After telling all the adults, we decided to wait to tell the kids, who were still young enough to be clueless about the math. We didn't want them to know that we screwed up the "first comes love, then comes marriage" order, so we decided to get married very early in my pregnancy so I didn't look like a Teletubby in our wedding photos. We had a very small wedding in the backyard of my mom and stepfather's house, with only close family members and a few close friends because we were short on time and even shorter on money, but aside from not being able to invite everyone we loved, I'll never regret how it worked out. The wedding was intimate and lovely, and because we weren't financially prepared to plan and execute a wedding in six weeks, many people who were family friends made extremely generous donations to make it happen. A family friend offered to do the photography, another one offered up a limo to pick us up after the ceremony, and yet another offered up her gorgeous lake house near my home town for us to stay after the wedding. A friend in Austin took my bridal portraits as a gift. Tim's brother and sister in-law donated the champagne. Our niece performed Irish step dancing at the little intimate backyard reception, and one of my best friends sang "Angel from Montgomery" as we danced our first dance. Mom got a sweet deal from her friends who have an Irish band, so they played beautiful Irish music during the reception. My sister took care of almost all of the planning, paid for our tent rentals, and helped save money by organizing the bridesmaids into any pale pink dress of their choice so they could buy dresses at thrift stores if they wanted. Our wedding rings were sterling silver James Avery bands that cost $27 each, and we each had a secret message engraved inside. Tim's says, "Put that back on!"

Okay, I'm kidding. I'm not telling you what it says. He never takes his ring off, so he doesn't know what it says, anyway.

At our wedding, Matthew was Tim's best man, and Stephanie

was my maid of honor. My sister Emily was the flower girl. My aunt Pat played the keyboard for the ceremony, and my uncle L.B., a retired county judge, married us. L.B. had performed countless weddings before ours, but he got nervous and accidentally skipped Tim's vows, so we weren't really sure if we were married or not. To be safe, the next morning at the lakehouse, Tim redid his vows on the dock as the sun was coming up. It was all very dreamy, and for some reason, even more special knowing that while all of the wedding excitement happened, I was growing a baby. I've always been a pretty decent multitasker.

After the wedding, we made plans to tell the kids about our growing family. I took the sonogram and put it in a frame, and we planned on giving it to the kids at breakfast. It's funny that I did that, because I think sonograms are so creepy, and I always think it's so weird that women plaster their sonogram pictures everywhere, like, "Hey! Looky here at the inside of my body! And look close! There's a little fertilized human egg in there!"

To share the news, Tim and I took the kids to a breakfast diner, and at some point during the pancake course, we let the kids open the bag with the framed sonogram in it. We kind of figured they wouldn't have a clue what the photo was about, but Stephanie is always two steps ahead of us.

"You're having a BABY?" Stephanie asked, half excited, half horrified.

Matthew just smiled shyly, his little dimples showing his approval.

"I like babies," he said.

Whew. We were out of the woods. Nobody lost their minds

or had a temper tantrum. Since I didn't want to find out the sex of the baby, we named the baby "Dot." It had some significance because my grandmother Dorothy went by Dot, and that's what it looked like on the sonogram picture.

We signed up for birthing classes, and Tim thought it was hilarious because in his eyes, if a couple opts out of birthing classes, a baby is still coming no matter what. What do you really need to know except in nine months, that baby is coming out? This is easy for Tim to say since he hasn't given birth before, but I do kind of see what he means.

The class was packed with upper-middle-class Austin couples, most of them first-time parents. On the Saturday where they showed the birthing video, Stephanie and Matthew were with us, so we brought them along. They had a little room with a television and a VCR to entertain the kids while the parents were in class, and to keep them from hearing traumatic things like "perineum" and "mucus plug." We sat on the floor as the birthing video began. At the very moment a woman with frighteningly long 70s pubic hair began pushing a human head out of her vagina, Stephanie came in the room to let us know the VCR tape was over. She sat in Tim's lap and watched along as the woman screamed for mercy and her vagina stretched to the size of a classroom globe. I'm not sure who was more traumatized, Stephanie, Tim, me, or the birthing class coach and students. Tim shuffled Stephanie out of the room while I fought back the urge to vomit or jump off a bridge. We got in the car and nobody talked about it and that was absolutely fine with me.

A few weeks later, we were at one of our favorite Mexican food restaurants for dinner. The kids were with us, and Matthew asked Tim to take him to the restroom. While Tim was gone, Stephanie used the opportunity to educate me.

She asked me, "Do you know what is going to happen when you have the baby?"

I waited for her to tell me about how cute the baby would be, or how she would be excited to hold her or help feed her or whatever little kids do when babies are born. The restaurant was rather crowded and because Stephanie is an Arndt, she is not a quiet kid. The Arndts are a loud people. It comes from generations of big Catholic families, where everybody has to yell to get anyone to listen to them.

"Well," she yelled. "YOUR VAGINA IS GOING TO GET THIS BIG." She held her arms up to the size of a manhole.

At the same time Stephanie was yelling this announcement loud enough for the dishwashers in the back room to hear, Tim and Matthew came out of the bathroom. Poor little shy Matthew probably wanted to die. Part of me thinks Stephanie kind of enjoyed the entire scene. At this point she wasn't fully fond of me, so I concluded that she took just a little bit of delight in scaring me to death. Now that I've had some time to back away from it, it's really a great story. The "Your Vagina is Going to Get This Big" is one of the most frequently told family stories at Tim's family holiday celebrations, because I married a man whose family talks about vaginas over Thanksgiving dinner.

All these years later, Tim and I know one thing is certain. We know birth control doesn't always do its job, but that a really good birth control method is to show your kids the birthing video. For extra impact, show it right before your high-school aged kids go out on dates. It just might work.

Allergic to Pregnancy

I'm not particularly religious now, but when it comes to my pregnancy, I think there was some divine intervention taking place. For starters, I was on the pill when I got pregnant. It can happen, ladies. If you don't want to get pregnant, you might want to consider just not having sex. That, or get on the pill, but also have an IUD, use a condom (come on, you should be doing that anyway), and have sex in a bathtub full of spermicide, just to be safe.

Having an unplanned pregnancy in Texas offers you an extra dose of guilt and pressure. Our old white male legislators have made a sport out of blocking women's reproductive health options, so their constant propaganda can really seep into your psyche. Never mind that it's a weird conversation to call your parents and announce that you are getting married in the same call where you deliver the news they are going to become grandparents. I consider it efficient multitasking, but at some point, I began to think that the universe set out to punish me for getting pregnant before I was married.

Stack up a list of all of the possible health issues a woman can have while pregnant, and I had most of them. It began with constant heartburn that was so relentless I had to sleep sitting straight up. I had two pregnancy cravings: fried chicken strips and peppermint milkshakes, and I gave into those cravings with regularity. The heartburn from that nonsense was so unbearable that, for Christmas that year, everyone gave me personalized stockings full of Tums. That was cute.

Later, when my otherwise dainty ankles turned into cankles, I was forced to venture out to our local outlet mall to purchase comfortable shoes because I certainly wasn't going to pay full price for comfortable shoes. With Tim in tow to feed me Tums and find places for me to sit and pant, I settled on a pair of Clark's slides. Up until that point in my life, I put a lot of focus on what I wore on my feet. The departure from kitten heels to Clark's slides made me feel like I'd swapped bodies with a high school women's basketball coach dressed for the Spring Awards Banquet. It was miserable, but my wounded ego wasn't the worst part. Just mere days later, the fashion universe decided to punish me further by making me allergic to Clark's slides. No matter what I did, I couldn't wear them without my feet turning the color of rotting raspberries and itching to the point where I cried in misery. While that was happening and I was scrambling around trying to find a shoe that didn't make me scratch my feet off, my feet also decided to grow half a size, forcing me to donate an entire closet worth of adorable size 9 shoes.

From there, I developed gestational diabetes. It was devastating news because it forced me to eat pea-sized portions, and the food plan forbade chicken strips and peppermint milkshakes. I got to poke myself with a needle poker gizmo to measure my blood sugar levels several times a day. I also got to waddle around the block with Tim after every meal. It ended up being a blessing in disguise, because I actually lost weight during my pregnancy and I looked pretty terrific after getting my eating under control.

From there, I got preeclampsia, which is a fancy word for pregnant lady high blood pressure. My blood pressure got so high it forced me into bed rest for three weeks. Those were the weeks I'd carefully planned to fully organize my home, purge years' worth of papers, and fully disinfect every nook and cranny in our house.

Some might think bed rest is a treat. I get that. Being ordered to bed under normal circumstances gives one the opportunity to binge watch Downton Abbey or HGTV for weeks and eat ginger-bread pancakes in bed while your partner licks syrup off of your boobs. But three weeks of bed rest while you have a genetically modified watermelon in your body is one of the most miserable experiences you can ever imagine. No matter how much Oprah I watched, the only thing I could really think about was getting that baby out of my body, and how that was going to go down. No matter how many books I read, or how many people I knew had successfully shoved giant watermelons out of their vaginas, there was just no way MY vagina was going to cooperate with that.

On the Monday of my last doctor's appointment before the due date, Tim helped heave me out of my nest into the SUV, at which point I was so enormous that the seat belt wouldn't even fasten and I was convinced the baby weighed at least 27 pounds. When the doctor saw me, she said,

"You're having this baby on Wednesday."

Wait. Two weeks early? No. No. I wasn't ready! I needed to order my husband around to disinfect our home and alphabetize my magazines! She sternly repeated herself and scheduled an induction for that Wednesday. Well, alrighty then.

So much of the following few days is a blur to me. What isn't a blur is my birthing plan. I would show you the exact copy, but apparently the charge nurse took one look at me, at the birthing plan, laughed out loud and pinned it up on the stupid little charge nurse bulletin board under the area reserved for "the most ridiculous birthing plans ever written." I remember some of it, though, because it was my BIRTHING PLAN and it was important. It went something like this:

- The mother would like low lighting and candles during labor.
- The mother would like a yoga ball on which to softly bounce during the uncomfortable moments of labor.
- The mother would like a string quartet gently playing Vivaldi to the beat of her contractions.
- The mother would like her stepchildren, parents, stepparents, and most of the family gently ushered out any time her vagina is exposed or discussed. Because really.
- No Pitocin.
- No epidurals.
- No C-sections.
- The mother would like high fives while she gently pushes the freakishly tiny but unbelievably healthy baby out of

her body, followed immediately by a mimosa and a back rub by a massage therapist who looks like Jude Law.

- The mother would like a quick makeup touch-up before the photos begin.

I really mean it when I'm telling you the charge nurse threw that plan away from the minute I checked in. Let me do my best to describe the charge nurse. She was pushing 350 pounds, most of it muscle. She was efficient and stern and there was no pushing back on her demands. She gave me Pitocin. I didn't have a say-so; we needed to induce the labor. She demanded that I stay on my left side to regulate my ever-rising blood pressure. Never mind that I was crying from being so sore. Never mind that the bed on which I was forced to stay on one side was very possibly a metal embalming table from the basement morgue.

The Pitocin was a bust. I think I had about 1 ½ contractions in total. Sorry, ladies. For some reason, I got the "easy" way out, I'm guessing because my entire pregnancy was so challenging. When they made the decision to break my water as the baby's heart rate was dropping and my blood pressure rose, the giant charge nurse flopped me onto my back, spread my legs, and broke my water with a giant knitting needle.

"Um, candles? String quartet?" I thought, but wisely said nothing as a tidal wave of warm weird birthing water drenched the metal table while my family watched in horror. I'm pretty sure my stepmother Pam took photos.

Man, giving birth is gross.

Meanwhile, Tim, who had already been through the birth of

his two older children, went home to get his kids ready for bed. Tim's first wife went through something like 170 hours of labor with both kids. She was a complete champ, according to legend, and birthed two perfect kids as a result of her skills. So it made sense that Tim would leave me at the hospital given that I wasn't even dilated to the size of a pencil eraser at that point. The plan was for Tim to swap places with my mother, who was there to see the birth of her first biological grandchild, but who was also being a saint and helping out with my stepchildren.

Never mind that I never got the appropriate amount of nesting time, I clearly wasn't the only one who needed some nesting. While I was getting intimate with the nurse with giant football glove hands, Tim took it upon himself to whip up a fresh batch of banana bread. Naturally, about the time Tim was in the comfort of our kitchen, whistling and sliding a baking pan into the oven while his fully formed kids frolicked around the house, the doctor determined that it was time for a C-section. Now, I was obviously out of it, but this seemed like a big conspiracy for my otherwise kind and sweet doctor to get to a movie that night, or run home for the evening news, because the announcement that it was "go" time happened very abruptly to me. Suddenly, my mother was throwing on scrubs and I was panicking. Where in the everloving hell was Tim? Was he going to MISS THE BIRTH OF OUR BABY? WHERE WAS MY MOTHER-EFFING BIRTHING PLAN?

I wasn't happy, but I didn't have time to get as livid as I wanted, because from there, it felt like a very dramatic episode of a television hospital drama. Beeps and beeps from the monitors, and my mom subbing in for Tim, which was all disturbing but also somewhat comforting given that Mom was a labor and delivery nurse in the 70s.

Somehow, as miracles go, Tim appeared in a cloud and he was fully scrubbed in and ready for show time. A lot of that memory has faded, but I do have a few distinct memories that might help those of you who end up having emergency C-sections. I may have been sleeping or eating Tums through the C-section part of my birthing class, but I don't recall ever hearing that they strap you down with your arms straight out at your sides when the surgery begins, and that you are absolutely not moving during the surgery. In other words, your nose better not itch because you aren't touching it. I also don't recall anyone saying that you could actually feel things. Think about how it feels when the dentist numbs your mouth and you accidentally bite your cheek. You have a bleeding mouth gash, but you really just feel a slight sensation. It's like that, but multiplied to the size of your entire lower body. During a C-section, it feels like you're buried in sand at the beach with your torso out in the world, but you can't move your arms, either, and then every few minutes you feel like something is weirdly tugging your insides out. And I guess that's what happening, except there's a baby down there.

I don't recommend the C-section. Obviously, plenty of us have them and I'm sure a large part of them are actually necessary. For years I wasn't really sure that mine was necessary, but it no longer matters. What's done is done. To this day, I carry around some really weird guilt about how I had a baby without doing any of the work. I literally didn't do the labor. I took weird medicine

I didn't really understand that didn't work, and next thing you know, the baby's heart rate is dropping and I'm strapped to a table and then I have a baby, but I don't get to hold her on my chest when she's goopy because they had to whisk her away to check her levels while the doctor put me back together. I was terrified, and because at this point you know my personality, you'll understand when the doctor gently said,

"Amy, you are going to need to stop talking now. You are bleeding a lot. We need to concentrate on sewing you back up."

That shut me up instantly, but all I wanted to do was scream, "Bring my baby to me! I believe at this point of my birthing plan, the baby should be on my chest right about now, and Cat Stevens or Yusef whatever his name is now should be in the room playing 'Wild World.' I also requested candles. Where are the unscented candles? And did somebody call the masseuse?"

In the end, the birthing plan didn't matter. What mattered was that on April 17, 2003, the baby was born. She was healthy. She was perfect.

The Plan was to name the baby after Tim's mother and my paternal grandmother, Dorothy. We had selected the name Dorothy Eileen, and tossed it around to the women we selected to be the baby's namesakes. We hadn't learned the sex of the baby, but we wanted to be sure we were set on the name in case she was a girl.

"Whatever you do, don't name the baby Dorothy," Granny Dorothy said. "For the rest of her life, people will compare her to Dorothy in 'The Wizard of Oz.'"

Oh.

"Whatever you do, don't name the baby Eileen," my mother in-law Eileen said. "Nobody can spell it."

Oh.

After they successfully stitched me up and I thankfully didn't die on the table, Tim brought the baby to me.

"Is this a Dorothy Eileen?" he asked, beaming. "I was showing her to the family through the glass but I didn't want to tell them her name just to be sure."

"No, she's an Emily Rose," I said, groggily. Her little rosy face looked just like my sister Emily. Also, I was on drugs.

That is how Emily Rose came to be. She named herself.

She really was perfect. I wasn't perfect, though. I was a mess. I was fully exhausted and traumatized over the weird fake labor, the emergency nature of the C-section, and my banana bread-making husband who nearly missed the whole deal. Once we were moved to our recovery room, I passed out and woke up in a dark room to see a glass incubator next to me with a sleeping baby in it. I remember looking at the baby and thinking, "Wait. I have to take THAT home with me?"

And then Al Pacino arrived.

The Nurse That Looked
Like Al Pacino

The baby arrived around 9pm. I will refer to her as the baby because from the first time I held her, I didn't have that maternal glow I was told I'd have. I'd forgotten to add "maternal glow" to my birthing plan. I knew I loved the baby, but I didn't have the natural bond you read about in the books. I was absolutely exhausted and completely overwhelmed.

When I say she arrived around 9pm, it's because I have no idea what the exact time of birth was. I know, I know, all good parents know the exact time their kid was born and how much they weighed and how long they were, and I can't remember any of these things. (For the record, I also don't know my wedding anniversary, so I'm not exactly good with the details.) We'd all been awake for many hours for my non-labor experience, so by the time I had a quick C-section, was sewn back together, had been through recovery and wheeled back to our room, I was completely wiped out.

Hospitals are not designed to give you time to rest. You're hooked up to all sorts of things and the beds are rock hard, and someone is waking you up every 15 minutes to poke on you, so a few hours after the birth, a nurse I mistook for a candy striper entered the room.

"Mrs. Arndt, I'm going to remove your catheter," she said timidly. The nurse couldn't have been over 16 years old, but there wasn't much I could do about it, so I spread my legs for the 35th time in less than 24 hours to another stranger. Childbirth means never worrying about showing your vagina off to strangers, so much that I'm kind of surprised women who have had babies don't just flash their vaginas during Mardi Gras. The preteen nurse got to work and within seconds, I felt like someone was pulling a cactus out of the place I normally pee.

"Ouch!" I screamed. "I'm sorry, but that really hurts."

Not sure why I apologized, but I did. She went at it again. And again, and for the first time in my life, felt like I understood what a man feels like to be kicked where it hurts.

"Ouch!" I screamed again. "Okay, I do not mean to be mean here, but could you please go get a nurse with experience?"

This was a pivotal moment for the Candy Striper. She could have been confident, and stated that she had experience, thank you very much, and would I please just be quiet while she worked? But instead, she ran out of the room, very possibly in tears. Moments later, the big water-breaking nurse entered the room with a sympathetic smile on her face.

"This is her first shift," she said. "I think she got a little nervous."

"Well," I said. "I appreciate a new person on their first day, but my vagina is not a practice field. It's also not a pin cushion."

Together, we laughed. Within seconds, that big lady effortlessly did whatever it takes to remove a catheter, only this time, I had no idea it was even happening. She was the skilled lover to Candy Striper's inexperienced teen fumbling. If you could dole out Yelp reviews for L&D nurses, I would have given her 5 stars.

"There," she said. "Everything should be better now."

I wanted her to stay forever. She was the big, strong, confident woman who arrived when I was afraid and in pain, and every time she came into the room, I felt a sense of safety and comfort. However, nurses do have to go home at some point.

This is when Al Pacino took over.

I never thought it was possible for a woman to look like Al Pacino, but if you consider that Dana Carvey looks exactly like Reba McIntyre, anything is possible. She was small and intense and had that same terrifying gaze, and when she spoke, she sounded *exactly* like Al Pacino. If I hadn't been waking up from abdominal surgery, I wouldn't have been able to control my laughter, but lucky for both of us, I was in no mood for a chuckle.

Al didn't mess around. She wasn't there to be friendly or to chat about pleasantries. For that reason alone, Al Pacino and Tim didn't stand a chance at clicking. Tim is all about pleasantries and small talk. Not Al. Al was a former military nurse and took her role as the night shift labor and delivery nurse extremely seriously.

Al Pacino knew her way around a breast. Before I even knew her real name, she had ripped open my gown and manhandled me in such an aggressive way that I wondered if she might be a freshman boy wearing an Al Pacino suit.

"We need to get your nipples ready to feed your baby," she

barked, pinching my nipples and twisting them around like she was trying to open a childproof medicine bottle.

She brought me the baby. I don't know if it was the weeks of sleep deprivation prior to the birth or the trauma of the C-section, but something inside me wasn't right. I still didn't feel that warm glowing halo of mother-child connection that I was supposed to be feeling. Al Pacino wasn't warm or glowing either, and for some reason, that comforted me.

"We need to get her to latch on," she growled.

The baby didn't latch. Al continued to assault my nipples, milking me like a cow, but nothing happened.

"We'll try again later."

She was disappointed. It was unclear if she was disappointed in me, the baby, or herself. This routine went on for what felt like days, and Al got to second base with me no less than seven hundred times during that first night shift. Slowly, Al was able to make a little of the pre-milk situation happen. Meanwhile, unbeknownst to me, the nurses in the nursery were conspiring against the cause, feeding the baby formula with a little finger feeder in the nursery while I recovered. Again, not on my birthing plan, but the baby needed to eat. I get it, even though I feel like the finger feeder was a big part of the problem. Babies are cute and all, but they are totally lazy. If someone was going to feed you with a tiny hose or force you to suck on a dry prune for hours, what would you choose? The baby loved being in the nursery where skilled baby holders catered to her every whim. The baby hated being shoved onto to my breast by an extremely irritated Al Pacino. Made sense to me.

Those first days in the hospital were a very weird time. I look back at family photos and don't even remember having guests, but there are pictures to prove that grandparents were there, and some close family friends, but outside of that, I don't remember much.

I do love all of the photos of my parents holding the baby, all glowing with their new titles as grandparents. I also love the photos of my stepchildren, who got scooped out of school to come see their new sister. I love that the second grade teacher, Mrs. Zarker, made a printed sign to post on the classroom door welcoming the baby to the world. The kids were so proud, and Tim and the kids even recreated a photo that they took when Stephanie was born, sitting on the floor of the hospital room, Tim in criss cross applesauce, holding the baby while her siblings stared at her in awe.

For me, there is one photo that I cling to - in it, I'm holding the baby and you can see a bond there. It's there, and it's faint, because quite frankly I didn't feel like it was happening at all. I am breathing in the smell of the baby. The photo doesn't show that inside, something wasn't right. You couldn't see the birth of the early phase of postpartum depression. It's not something you can see. And while it's something you can feel, if you don't know what to expect, you don't know how to describe it. For that reason alone, I really want someone to write *What To Expect When You Are Getting Postpartum Depression*. That would have been way more beneficial than the books about breast pumps and rubbing extra virgin olive oil on your hoo ha.

At one point, I cried in front of Al Pacino, fully frustrated that instead of bonding with my baby, I was waking up to the pain of the C-section and feeling like I couldn't handle any of it. Al let down her guard and was kind to me. She told me that I needed to trust her. That she has been a nurse for a very long time, and that she knew that her military background made her tough, but that for new moms, sometimes tough love is the best approach. It's what she knew.

Somehow, after a few days of boob groping, being woken every 17 minutes to get my levels checked, and after proving to the nurses that I could pee without exploding, it was time to go home. Someone went to our house (I'm guessing my mom), and brought a perfect little white outfit for ER to wear home. It had a sweet little bonnet, and it felt very much like we were taking home a doll, only that doll was actually alive. I smiled for the photos, but inside, I was screaming for help.

I wasn't ready for what came next.

So Much More Than the Baby Blues

When we came home from the hospital with the baby, I knew that being exhausted was normal, but something about me was still really off-kilter. The thing that's so hard about diagnosing any postpartum issues is that your first time around, there is absolutely no way to know what is normal and what is a sign that things are very wrong. For me, the first indication that something was wrong was that mere days after coming home from the hospital, I developed an intense desire to cook a meal for my entire family. And by meal, we're not talking about heating up a frozen lasagna served on paper plates while the family ooed and ahed over the baby. Rather, I had an overpowering need to orchestrate a sit-down dinner with my father, stepmother, and grandparents. This is highly unusual for a new mother recovering from a C-section, but even more unusual for me since Tim is our cook and I never make huge production meals.

In a slightly manic state, I whipped together a pretty complex meal of roast pork tenderloin, homemade garlic mashed potatoes, veggies, and a fancy salad. I set a beautiful table with wine in Waterford goblets, candles, the whole bit. Nobody in my family needed this, but I convinced myself that I needed to do it. It was almost as if I had reverse nesting since the bed rest had prevented me from engaging in my nesting activities. It was very weird. I was very weird, but I assumed this was normal, and that that was what new moms were supposed to do.

The next indication that things were off was that I started feeling really angry about the people around me. I remember Stephanie sitting beside me on the couch and wanting to be near the baby, and I had to hold back from yelling at her to leave us alone. All she was doing was being a sweet kid interested in being near her new sister, but I felt like when someone was sitting next to me it was suddenly 25 degrees hotter in the house.

My mother stayed with us to help out, and she was a huge help, but I was completely insensitive to her feelings. At one point, when the baby was screaming, Mom said,

"Aw, she's hungry."

At which point I barked, "Then whip out your huge tit and feed her!"

Mom ran out of the room and went to the front porch to cry while I sat emotionless wondering what the big deal was, and who was going to step up and finger feed the baby. Tim went outside and had a gentle conversation with my mother to let her know we had it covered, and that it was time for her to go home.

Only we didn't have it covered. I was beyond exhausted, and wasn't sure why things weren't starting to feel normal again. I had two default feelings: I either walked around in a haze, or I was extremely agitated. Most of all, I was very agitated with the baby, who wouldn't hang out on my breast for more than about 12 seconds.

Somewhere along the path to an emergency C-section and having to bring a live baby home with us, we missed some vital instructions about the breastfeeding. While I was recovering, the nurses were finger-feeding the baby in the nursery, and Al Pacino was trying to milk me to get things going. What everyone forgot to tell us (or we failed to hear, most likely the case) was that we were supposed to stop finger-feeding the baby when we got home. Since we missed that extremely relevant detail, I have some very sweet pictures of my kids feeding the baby with the little tiny bottle of formula and the tiny little tube that the baby preferred to my aching boobs.

We hired a lactation consultant who happened to be the mother of one of Stephanie's school friends. She came to the house and futzed around with my breast. She was less aggressive and scary than Al Pacino. With her help, I was able to get a little few semi-successful breastfeeding sections going, but I was still competing with that stupid finger feeder and it was winning hands-down.

By Mother's Day, which was a few weeks after the baby was born, she weighed less than when she was born. I have a photo of the two of us on Mother's Day, and the infant in that photo is so thin that I can't look at the picture without crying. Without realizing it, I was starving my own child.

It's no wonder she cried constantly. It's no wonder that I was feeling like a failure at parenting. Looking back, it all makes sense, but at the time, I was doing my best to put on a happy face and just handle what I thought was normal postpartum exhaustion.

We bought a breast pump at the advice of the doctors to help get the milk going, while supplementing with formula so the baby could thrive. I would hook myself up to the pump where I was urged to relax. Nearly an hour at the pump would only produce about 4 drops of milk. Meanwhile, I had friends with babies who were complaining about how they didn't have enough room in their freezers to hold all of the extra milk.

When the baby was less than a month old, we took a trip to Dallas to attend my niece's confirmation, and in the car, I felt like my breasts had caught on fire.

"Pull over," I ordered Tim. "I think I need to feed her."

I yanked my shirt to the side and put the baby on my breast, and for the first time, I felt my body provide nourishment for my daughter. While it wasn't the gentle glow that mothers describe when breastfeeding works properly, I felt relaxed for the first time since she was born. I touched her face and watched her gulp down actual breast milk, and I cried.

That day, the baby became Emily Rose. She was my baby. I loved her, and though we were having a rough time of it, we were going to be okay.

———

I assumed the feeling of contentment and near euphoria would last, but the anxiety and depression crept back in when I least expected it. I had good days and bad days, and though I wasn't counting, the bad days outnumbered the good ones. I remember trying to shake it off and wondering why I didn't have the power to make that happen.

Back at home, Tim went back to work and I stayed at home to figure out how to be a mother. When she cried, she was the baby. When she took her long naps and I could watch her sleeping, she was Emily Rose. Every emotion I felt was extremely intense. I tried to get out of the house as much as possible, because I felt great comfort in having other people around. I worried I would have a panic attack and die while trying to take care of my newborn.

One rainy afternoon, the baby was howling and I was home alone, trying to get her to breastfeed. Aside from the one incredible experience in the car on the way to Dallas, breastfeeding just wasn't working out. I gave up easily in favor of the bottle because I was so defeated. As the rain belted our little stone house, the baby screamed louder, and then our electricity went off. I sat in the dark room in our overstuffed Pottery Barn chair, holding the red-faced crying baby, and a wave of panic set in. It would never quit raining. The baby would never quit crying. I was terrified, and I was angry. I hated everything. At that moment, I had detailed fantasies of setting an alarm in the middle of the night and driving into the desert in my red Ford Explorer. I sat in the chair, planning my escape. But the sounds of the screaming baby got in the way, and I became desperate.

I picked up the phone to call Tim at work. I had to call Tim before something drastic happened. He answered on the first ring.

"Come home right now," I said. "Come home, or I am going to throw the baby."

No More Roasted Nuts: No More Plastic Toys

I didn't throw the baby.

I know. I know. I can't even find the adequate words to describe how thankful I am that I didn't throw the baby. After all of these years, I can't think about that day without crying and feeling a million knots in my stomach, knowing that I was that close to doing something so terrible and so drastic. I felt like a monster. That terrible day is the darkest day of my life, and for many years, I kept that day a secret. It was too dark, too terrible, too frightening for me to think of being in such a desperate place that I might have harmed my own child.

When I made the call to Tim, he must have driven 100 miles an hour in the rain to get home to us, because Tim is a hero. He came in, took the baby, and called my mom. He also called the OB. I don't know what happened in those conversations, but within what seems like mere hours, I was in my OB's office, explaining what I was feeling, and blowing it off as if it were nothing.

"I'm fine," I said. "I'm just exhausted."

"You are exhausted," Dr. Schmidt said. "And you also have postpartum depression. We are going to put you on medication to help you through this."

"Oh, I don't need medication," I said. "I'm just tired."

It probably went back and forth like this for a while until Tim and Dr. Schmidt were able to convince me that I needed the help. Denial can be extremely powerful when your hormones are raging like a 13-year old girl with PMS crossed with a menopausal woman who just had the world's most intense and powerful hot flash.

Boy, did I need the help. Until then, I had never taken an antidepressant in my life, and to that point, I had hardly taken medicine at all. I'm weirdly hippie about putting pharmaceuticals into my body, but it was definitely time. Dr. Schmidt prescribed a low dose of Zoloft, which I can now say is the most fabulous drug on the entire planet, because in a matter of days, I felt like a completely different person. The agitation subsided. The panic attacks disappeared. I was able to manage daily tasks without melting down.

Around the same time, my grandpa Glenn had been dealing with depression on his end. In his late 80s, Grandpa was pissed at the world that his body wouldn't allow him to play as much golf, and getting old was making him agitated and sad. He was also prescribed Zoloft, and when my father learned that I was dealing with depression, he told me about Grandpa. So I called Grandpa to discuss it.

"Take the goddamned pills!" Grandpa yelled into the phone. "I'm taking the pills, and that medicine has completely changed my "altitude." Grandpa was always full of frank advice and corny jokes. For some reason, knowing my own grandfather was getting some help from a little pill made me feel less shame about doing it myself. So what if two separate generations of Underwoods popped a little Zoloft? We needed it.

Thanks to Zoloft, my altitude also changed. Everything seemed to shift back into focus. Pre-Zoloft and at the peak of my postpartum depression, I remember looking at people and wondering why their heads were so big compared to their bodies, or why their eyes were so far apart. My perspective on everything was out of whack.

After I had a few days of medication in my system, Tim drove me to my hometown with Emily Rose. My treasure of a mom, who had been cast out of my house just a few weeks prior, helped get me back on my feet. She watched Emily Rose while I slept and slept. She fed me home cooked meals. She let me cry, and she listened to me when I needed to talk. She helped me with everything so I could manage life again. Between Tim, the OB, my mom, and many other family members and friends, I managed to survive.

When I returned to Austin, part of my routine was to have a regular visit with a psychiatrist, an ancient old codger who had a receptionist close to the doctor's age who might as well have been chain smoking Pall Malls behind the reception glass. The office was dark and masculine and smelled like stale smoke and mothballs. Since I was feeling so much better, I had to hold back from laughing as I eavesdropped on the receptionist's conversations with patients. It was a quirky place and I wondered how I'd gotten to the point where I needed to go there, but I was up for anything to feel better.

On my first meeting with the psychiatrist, we didn't talk about my postpartum depression. Quite frankly, I don't think that poor man had a clue in the world how to do that. However, he gave me one bit of advice that I'll never forget.

"Whatever you do, don't eat roasted nuts."

"I'm sorry?"

"Roasted nuts. Don't eat them."

The kooky old doctor launched into an endless conspiracy theory where the hypothesis was something about how the consumption of roasted nuts led to anxiety and depression. I sat huddled in his huge brown leather couch and listened intently. I believed every word he said to the point so much that I don't think I ate as much as a single almond for the next five years.

Flash to 13 years later, when I was selling chairs to a guy on Craigslist. The guy happened to be a psychiatrist named Stan, so I brought up the geezer psychiatrist and the roasted nuts. Stan wrinkled his nose and said he had never heard of this, and surely that couldn't be true. He was so rattled by this notion that he asked for my email so that he could look into it further, and a few days later, he wrote me back with this:

"I checked the literature and I didn't see anything convincing enough to make me warn others about the hazards of roasted nuts. But hey, I'm sure there's a study out there somewhere!"

Hey, I'm really quite sure there isn't!

But at the time, I was so desperate that I believed everything and desperately wanted to be "cured" from my anxiety and depression, so I avoided roasted nuts, even though I think the most roasted nut in this scenario was my psychiatrist.

As time passed and the Zoloft had enough time to completely kick in, I started feeling good enough to venture out into the world a bit more. I took Emily Rose to the park and pushed her in the baby swing and let her play in the grass. I took long walks in the neighborhood, fearful of having an anxiety attack but comforted by the familiar houses where I could ask for help if I needed it.

One day at the park, I ran into a neighbor who was a new mom as well. She had just given birth, and was already back to her fighting weight of 93 pounds. She's the kind of mom who runs marathons while pregnant, and gives birth while doing squats. I told her I'd been having a rough time, and she invited me to join her at a parenting group.

"It's a great way to bond with other moms," she said, gleefully breastfeeding her infant while her toddler waited patiently for his turn on her breast. "You should come!"

I figured it couldn't hurt, so I agreed to meet her there. I packed up plenty of premixed formula for Emily Rose, who was fattening up quite nicely and becoming really fun to tote around. I loaded her up in her carseat and drove to the place where the parenting group was held, a conference room in a small local library branch. When I arrived, I instantly regretted not asking my neighbor what kind of parenting group this was. The sign on the whiteboard outside the room pointed to my nightmare:

"Attachment Parenting Group: 12:00."

Uh-oh. Somewhere during the conversation with my neighbor,

I missed the part about attachment parenting. Now, before I offend many people, let me say this. There are all different kinds of parenting methods, and I'm certain that they all have benefits for different families. I am all for new parents figuring out what works for them. For some, letting the kid howl and cry in their crib while the parents sit outside patting themselves on the back for their strength is totally okay for those families. Tim and I were not that kind of parents. We preferred to let a mere squeak from Emily Rose launch us into a completely guilt-ridden exercise where one or both of us picked her up immediately and coddled her. We kept that up until she was in about 7th grade.

At the attachment parenting meeting, I nervously entered the room where a half dozen or so women sat on the floor, peacefully cuddling their calm babies who were literally attached to their bodies in slings. I waddled in, carrying Emily Rose in a 52-pound car seat bucket. I immediately reached into my bag and pulled out a fresh bottle of formula, while one of the moms looked at me with a sad expression and said,

"Oh, you're not breastfeeding?"

That alone was enough to make me turn around and leave, but I was meeting my friend there, so I simply said,

"Nope. Not in the cards for us."

From there, I pulled Emily Rose out of the car seat and held her in my arms, sheepishly giving her the bottle while the other moms began to whip out their milk-filled breasts to feed their happy little cherubs. They all looked at me with a mixture of pity and concern. One mother, a woman with blonde dreadlocks circled in a cloud of patchouli whipped out a nipple the size of an iPhone and shoved it in her infant's mouth. Two seconds later, her other child who was old enough to ride a bike ran in and pushed on her other breast while she smiled and said/sang something like,

"It looks like you're wanting milk, Nolan. When Ryder is finished, you can have your turn. Thanks!"

I somehow resisted the urge to smack her in the face. It reminded me of when my mom was at a meeting once years and years ago, and a kid walked into the room, pushed on her mom's chest, and said, "Milk, mama, milk!"

When mom told us the story, although she has plenty of hippie tendencies, she said, "I'm sorry, but if the kid is old enough to go to the refrigerator and get their own milk, it's time to stop breastfeeding."

I totally agree. Some of you will hate me for this, but there comes a point where if you have to make appointments to breastfeed your kid at the elementary school, perhaps you should just send them some organic milk boxes and call it a day.

The group leader came in and invited us to introduce ourselves. I don't even remember what the session topic was because within the hour, the following things happened:

- A mom turned to me and said, "We only use wooden toys. Plastic toys are really toxic." She said this as Emily Rose chewed on a plastic Elmo.
- A mom talked about the dangers of formula while I sat feeding my baby formula.

- A mom talked about how babies can't self-soothe while Emily Rose wailed, and I seriously considered asking the woman with the dreadlocks to breastfeed my kid.

My sweet neighbor meant well when she invited me to this group, but all it did was cause me to haul my gigantic plastic car seat across the parking lot, turn on the car while Emily Rose screamed, and burst into big ugly tears for about half an hour before gathering up enough energy to drive us both home. I felt more like a loser than ever before. I couldn't breastfeed, so I was a failure. I couldn't coerce my wiggly baby to fit inside one of those weird cocoon slings, so I was a failure. I had plastic toys all over my house, and no money to replace them all with wooden toys, so I was a failure. I might as well have taken up prostitution and crack use, except for I was still a little numb from the waist down and I worried that the crack might counteract the Zoloft.

And did I mention that I was doing all of this while also learning how to be a stepmother?

Joseph was the Original Stepfather

I've always thought that one of the most unbelievable stories is how Jesus came to be. If you grew up Christian like the rest of us from East Texas, from the moment you could attend Vacation Bible School, you heard account after account of the story of Jesus' birth. If it's been a few years since you reviewed the biblical version, or if you're one of my non-Christian friends, let's take a minute to review it together, because I'm sorry, but it's absolutely hilarious to me. When I was little, I thought the Bible was the most boring book on the planet, but as an adult, going back and reading this story, it's really quite juicy.

Here it is:

> In the sixth month of Elizabeth's pregnancy, God sent the angel Gabriel to Nazareth, a town in Galilee, to a virgin pledged to be married to a man named Joseph, a descendant of David. The virgin's name was Mary. The angel went to her and said, "Greetings, you who are highly favored! The Lord is with you."

Mary was greatly troubled at his words and wondered what kind of greeting this might be. But the angel said to her, "Do not be afraid, Mary; you have found favor with God. You will conceive and give birth to a son, and you are to call him Jesus. He will be great and will be called the Son of the Most High. The Lord God will give him the throne of his father David, and he will reign over Jacob's descendants forever; his kingdom will never end."

"How will this be," Mary asked the angel, "since I am a virgin?"

The angel answered, "The Holy Spirit will come on you, and the power of the Most High will overshadow you. So the holy one to be born will be called the Son of God. Even Elizabeth your relative is going to have a child in her old age, and she who was said to be unable to conceive is in her sixth month. For no word from God will ever fail."

"I am the Lord's servant," Mary answered. "May your word to me be fulfilled." Then the angel left her.

Is that not the craziest story ever written? It's completely unreal, and yet it's also the ultimate sales pitch:

"He will be great." If I were Mary, I think I would have laughed out loud at that part. I'd be thinking, "Look, Angel Gabriel, I didn't ask for this baby, but he's the *son of God*. He freaking better be great! You don't really need to sell him to me at this point. It sounds like I don't have much of a choice here anyway."

"Even Elizabeth your relative is going to have a child in her old age." What was Mary supposed to say to that? "Um, thanks? Just because my old relative is pregnant well past menopause, that's not exactly the motivation I need to get pregnant myself. Quit trying to rationalize this ridiculous situation. I haven't even had sex yet! This is not the way this works, Gabe."

Let's take this out of the Biblical context and break it down.

First, you have Mary, a young virgin, who gets an unexpected middle of the night wake-up call from an angel, letting her know that despite the fact she's a virgin, she's going to get knocked up with God's baby.

But wait! Mary's engaged to Joseph.

And if this weren't shocking enough for Mary, let's look at this situation from Joseph's perspective, because it is *really* messed up. Can you imagine what Joseph must have thought when Mary dropped that bomb?

"Hey, Joseph. You may want to sit down for this one. *Crazy* story. Last night, an angel woke me up, and - get this - I'm going to have God's baby."

"Wait, what?"

"I know! It's nuts, right? Evidently God is going to have a son, and I'm going to be the mom. Like a surrogate."

"And who exactly is this 'God'?"

"The real one! *The Most High.*"

"Somebody's high here, that's for damned sure. So, let me

get this straight. You're going to have sex with God? Oh, I'm sure THAT will be mind-blowing."

"No, the crazy thing is that I'll still be a virgin! No sex involved whatsoever, if you can believe that. It was a pretty quick conversation so we didn't work out the details."

Joseph stands up and paces around a bit, tugging on his beard.

"Mary, I need to step out for a minute. This is absolute balderdash. You're getting pregnant with God's baby. You. The virgin. First, Elizabeth, a woman who's old enough to be our grandmother gets pregnant and now *this*? This is rich, Mary. This is really rich."

He storms off, slams the thatched door, and heads off down the dirt path. From there, I'm pretty sure Joseph takes a long walk where he laughs and cries and shouts Biblical era obscenities. After some time, he ends up bellied up to the bar at the local Nazarene corner watering hole where he drinks a lot of mead or whatever they drank back then. I'm guessing Joseph drinks for hours, alternating between crying and explaining to friends and perfect strangers that his woman had plans to hook up with someone she described as God, and she was going to have "God's" baby. The "Lord's servant" and all. The guys pat him on the back and shake their heads. Poor schmuck Joseph.

Yet, somehow, Joseph sobers up and decides to stand by his lady. Merely for this action alone, I have always felt that Joseph is one of the most underrated people in the bible because who does that? Who decides to have enough faith to believe that his virgin girlfriend is still a virgin but about to be pregnant with God's kid? For starters, he had to decide quickly if he should run for the hills and get as far away from Mary as possible, or if he's going to go with the flow and stay by Mary's side as she gives birth to the son of God.

We don't get many details on Joseph's reaction, if any at all. Was he angry? Did he threaten to leave? Or did he just have blind faith and say, "Sounds great, Mary. Let's do this. Let's raise this kid and I'll treat him as if he's my own because clearly, I'm destined to be the stepfather to the son of God."

As history goes, Joseph was the original stepfather, and he deserves endless praise for stepping up for that gig. I can't imagine he felt adequate about it. We don't hear stories of Jesus rolling his eyes when Joseph told him to clean his room or help with the dishes. We don't get to hear any accounts of Joseph wondering how Jesus felt about their relationship, or if at any point in history, Jesus yelled at Joseph, "You're not my father! You can't tell me what to do!"

Of course I have a soft spot in my heart for Joseph because there are two kinds of people in this world: stepparents and people who are not stepparents. For me, when I have step-parenting challenges, instead of asking, "What Would Jesus Do?" I ask myself what Joseph would do. Jesus was the son of God and the Prince of Peace and all of that good stuff, but the one thing Jesus wasn't was a stepparent. But I sure hope Jesus appreciated that Joseph decided to stick around. I also hope that when Jesus was doing the carpentry gig, he carved out a wooden sign for Joseph for Father's Day that said, "Best Stepfather," because Lord knows Joseph deserved it.

Confessions of a Girl Scout Cookie Mom

As much as I would love to tell you that I'm the kind of working mother who has her act together, it's simply not the case. I'm the mom who keeps a razor in her car because inevitably, I'll be driving to a meeting and look down and realize I have one hairy knee, because I don't even have my act together enough to remember to shave both knees. When a school party sign-up list goes up and all of the other parents work hours cutting fresh fruit into the shape of the school mascot, I sign up to bring napkins. That way, if I forget the napkins (and believe me, I will), the kids won't starve, and they can just wipe their messy little hands on their clean little pants.

It's not that I haven't tried to be the kind of mom who has her act together. When Stephanie was in elementary school, I stepped up to be the Girl Scout Cookie Mom. Looking back, I'm pretty convinced that one of the other moms drugged me and got me to say yes, while all of the other moms laughed wickedly behind my back. After all, I was a fairly new stepparent. That alone automatically made me feel like a second class citizen, and at that point in my life, I didn't know The Secret to Being a Cookie Mom. Now that I know the secret, I'm going to share it with you. Considering being a cookie mom? Grab a box of Do-Si-Dos and a glass of milk and sit down for a lesson. If you've been a Cookie Mom before, I will enjoy having a glass of wine with you in God's special spa retreat in Heaven, because we will deserve it. If you haven't been a Cookie Mom, let's start with the job description:

> *Wanted: Cheerful, naive sucker. Must pass a background check that rivals the FBI and CIA combined. Requirements include attending training sessions with instructors who wear Christmas sweaters in June and being willing to gain 10 pounds during Cookie Sale. Candidates must own a minivan and be proud of it. Should delight in outdated, inefficient business practices. Must have space in your home to house a minimum of 1,500 cases of cookies. Should own a dolly, a strong husband, or both. The ideal candidate will possess the physical and emotional strength to fight off their strong husband with a stick when he cracks open cases labeled for other kids and eats Thin Mints while laughing maniacally.*

> *The candidate will graciously manage mothers who appear organized, but inevitably show up two hours late to pick up cookies at the same time they have stripped down to their bra and panties in the hopes of diving into a hot bath. Scheduling consideration*

*during the Cookie Sale: Be prepared to call in sick
to work at least once to cry uncontrollably while
counting piles of loose change.*

I'm telling you, the loose change alone should make you panic. I had so much money to handle I felt like I was in a scene in *Scarface*, minus the gritty, gangster glamour. Instead of sitting at a table with stacks of cash, I was slumped in our overstuffed Pottery Barn chair buried in nickels, dimes and quarters, shoving cookies down my gullet, scribbling illegible notes on post-its, trying to learn Accounting 101 while warding off an extended visit to our local mental health facility. But damn, I was a good stepmother! The other mothers were SO impressed by my Girl Scout spirit!

Don't get me wrong; I completely appreciate what the Girl Scouts do for our young girls. Both of my daughters had a blast doing it, and the mothers who volunteered to take on the meetings are getting extra complimentary spa treatments at God's spa retreat in heaven. The Girl Scouts teach sisterhood, female empowerment, and basic finance. During the cookie sale, girls learn about customer service (a lost art), door-to-door sales (that's a little scary), and how to handle rejection. Good lessons, all.

The next time you stroll past a cookie booth, please buy some cookies. Who cares if they're loaded with calories and ridiculously overpriced? You'll help a local troop keep a fraction of the profits, make a kid smile, but most of all, you'll make that Cookie Mom feel worthwhile. And if you're really feeling charitable, write a check for the exact amount, please. The Cookie Mom will thank you.

Doing the Math

A t some point, it was bound to come up.

From the moment I realized I was pregnant with Emily Rose, Tim and I became masters of the sleight of hand. We pulled off the wedding just six weeks after telling close friends and family the dealio. We also managed to work it so that Matthew and Stephanie would have in their heads that in our story, we lined up rather well with the "First Comes Love, Then Comes Marriage" storyline.

At the wedding, my mother in-law Eileen, who was in her mid-70s at the time, had such a great time that when the Irish band launched into a rendition of the "Cotton-Eyed Joe," she hooked arms with my mother and sister in-law and danced so hard that I laughed so hard I thought I might explode. Given that I was pregnant, I didn't have the excuse of being even the slightest bit tipsy; it was just so terrific to see Eileen dancing with that much passion, her svelte little legs rocking the back patio-turned wedding reception dance floor. I laughed harder and harder, unable to control it because it was so ridiculously funny to me, and before I knew it, I was also unable to control my bladder.

Stephanie, ever the astute observer, followed me into the

bathroom where I was still laughing uncontrollably and begging Tim to pull off my Spanx. Spanx are at the same time the best and worst invention in the world, and really should come with a warning that pregnant brides not wear them, but I was the bride and rather vain and didn't want my newly pregnant bump showing, so I made the call to wear them. And then I peed in them because that's how pregnant brides roll.

As Tim awkwardly peeled me out of my peepee Spanx, Stephanie watched on, completely amused, and suddenly I heard her shout to all of the guests,

"Amy peed her wedding dress! Amy peed her wedding dress!"

I may as well come out with it and let you know that the peeing in the wedding dress incident was easily the 527th time in my life I've wet my pants. It began in 2nd grade in the school cafeteria at lunch, when Trey Stephens, the cutest boy with the perfect hair and the bright white smile grabbed a pickle from his lunch box, held it up and said in his perfect little Matthew McConaughey East Texas drawl:

"This pickle looks like a dick!"

What's so funny about that is that I'm certain that I had absolutely no idea what a dick was at that point, but it came from the mouth of Trey Stephens, so it didn't matter. All of the kids circled around our lunch table burst into a huge fit of 2nd grade giggles, and because I wanted Trey to know just how funny he was, I punctuated the laughter by dropping my head onto the table and conking a huge knot on my forehead. That made us all laugh even harder, and before I knew it, I was peeing a puddle on the Andy Woods Elementary School cafeteria floor.

The teachers realized what was happening when everyone at my table and bordering tables began to laugh and point at the puddle and then at me. One of the teachers had the bright idea to usher me out by holding a lunchbox in front of my pants, and hold another one to the back in an effort to provide some kind of invisible force field as they scooted me out of the cafeteria. From there, it's all a little post traumatic stressish and blurry, but remember Mr. Lauderdale with the glass paddle? Well, he evidently had a soft spot for kids who peed on the floor, because somehow he let me stay home for at least a day, if not two, it's hard to remember. Also, much later in life, a kid admitted to me that my teacher Mrs. Booker told the class that I had an accident and that nobody was to talk about it when I returned. It's actually crazy to imagine how much attention I got for peeing on the floor (which may explain why I continued to do it for the rest of my life).

But, lest you think Mrs. Booker is a hero for talking to the kids about The Cafeteria Incident, that woman also had a crazy mean streak. Once, she ran around dramatically spraying Lysol all around a poor little boy named Barney as she proclaimed, "Barney farted! Ooh, boy. Barney farted." Mrs. Booker wasn't exactly a saint is what I'm saying.

For the remainder of my life, whenever things got really funny, I peed my pants. Like the time when Christi Cole and I were playing in a pop-up camper with her big brother Doug and his friend Lance, and Lance was a bit on the husky side, and he sat on one side of the camper, which wasn't fastened to the ground, and we all went rolling over to the Lance side and toppled the entire camper over on its side. I mean, I'm sorry, but we laughed so hard that surely I wasn't the only one who peed a little. It was pee in your pants funny!

I tell you all of this not because I enjoy reliving my countless tales of childhood incontinence, but because it all leads to the fact that it's only really part of why I peed in my wedding dress. I was six weeks pregnant, and thank goodness Matthew and Stephanie didn't have the elementary school wherewithal to do the math and realize that on the day they received a new stepmother, a baby wasn't far behind.

I never expected that by the time Emily Rose started getting sex education in the public schools that she would consider that Tim and I had an October anniversary and she was born in April. It just never crossed my mind. So imagine my surprise when one day when Emily Rose was ten, we were in the car headed who knows where when she suddenly said,

"Mommy, was I at your wedding?"

"I'm sorry?"

"Was I there. Like on the day you married Daddy."

"Well, of course you were. You've always been with me. You started as an egg.." I began.

"I'm not asking THAT," she said firmly. "I"m asking if Daddy's sperm was inside you and I was in your belly on your wedding day."

Damn, girl! From there, I was forced to have the real deal conversation with Emily Rose, and I handled it really well if I do say so myself. It went a little something like this:

"Yes, you were there on our wedding day. The best thing about that day was it was the best day of my life. You can ask

Daddy how crazy and chaotic the wedding was, but when the moment came for us to stand before Uncle L.B. and recite our vows, we felt like we were the only people in the world, yet also surrounded by so much love. Matthew and Stephanie were there, and so were you, and you were the reason our family came together, so I wouldn't have wanted it any other way."

She smiled. This news seemed to satisfy her and melt away any of the negative connotations of an East Texas shotgun wedding. Meanwhile, I sat mentally patting myself on the back for coming up with the perfect response to an otherwise mortifying question.

I don't know why I thought that Tim and I would actually be able to keep the mathematical details out of the storyline forever, because at the end of the day, it didn't matter anyway. So our storyline changed a little: First comes love, then comes positive pregnancy test, then comes wedding, then comes instant family, then comes baby. And with the birth of our little tiebreaker, the family was complete.

The Lice Survival Kit

Even though my childhood friend Dawn warned us about lice with her serious advice about not wearing someone else's hat, I'm pretty sure we all have to deal with lice at some point in our kids' lives. I know that finding out your kid has lice feels like one of the worst things that can happen to a family, but I'm here to tell you that if that's the worst thing that happens to you, you're really going to be just fine. It's nasty, but you'll be okay. I'm no entomologist, but in my experience there are two types of kids: the kind that lice love, and the kind that lice ignore. I won't reveal which of my three kids ended up in the latter category, but let's just say that's the kid who didn't have long hair.

The first time the school called to let us know about a lice outbreak, Emily Rose was in preschool. I'd first like to state for those of you who are big snobs that lice do not discriminate and lice don't just go to "dirty" daycares. Emily Rose's daycare was so ridiculously expensive that when we enrolled her in public kindergarten we felt like we'd gotten a huge raise. Lice go anywhere kids go, and since adults don't seem to lay on each other and hug each other non-stop, lice tend to be primarily a kid's problem that adults get to try and solve.

The first time the school called us to let us know Emily Rose had lice, I immediately began experiencing phantom itching from head to toe. Tim, a much less dramatic sort, got busy doing load after load of laundry. He fought off our terrorized preschooler as he shoved 14,000 stuffed animals into garbage bags for a week-long vacation to our garage. I called my sister Emily, who has gone above and beyond to help me with parenting emergencies countless times, and invited her to come over for a lice-removal party. She showed up even though she has the thickest hair in our family and put herself at great risk. God bless that woman.

Once, the school got a big lice outbreak around Halloween, and I wasn't convinced I'd gotten the entire job done (in the beginning, you really never know) and so I sent Emily Rose off to a costume party, her hair slathered in mayonnaise in a shower cap, and on top of that, she had on a bright pink wig. That must have been the single most miserable Halloween of Emily Rose's life except for the year she asked us to wrap her like a mummy. That year, my saintly sister painstakingly wrapped Emily Rose from head to toe in white material strips because that's what the kid wanted. But once we got to the school and she spotted everyone else dressed in Disney princess and cheerleading costumes, Emily Rose burst into tears and begged us to take her home and let her change clothes.

The worst lice story I know is that a dad at my kid's elementary school who had a reputation for being a complete weirdo had twin girls, and instead of handling the lice, he just shaved their poor little heads completely bald, and then sent them to school in terrible wigs so they looked like old women. Since it's Texas, those poor girls were not only miserable from being bald twins in wigs, they were also sweaty bald twins in wigs. I wish someone would have thumped that father, or forced him to shave his head and wear a wig with a coworker that looked a lot like him. Such a bad parenting move, man.

This is a list that I consider a must-have for families who are battling lice for the first time. Lucky for me, my kids have passed the age of getting lice (at least I hope so), so when parents with little ones come to me with lice horrors, I can always put them at ease.

Lice Survival Kit

- LED flashlight
- White bowl of hot water
- Metal drugstore lice comb (with very thin teeth)
- Prescription lice shampoo
- Disney Channel
- Industrial-sized container of laundry soap
- Four-pack of couple's counseling appointments
- Case of red wine

The comb is what you'll use to comb through every strand of your kid's hair. The flashlight works wonders for finding eggs and bugs if you spot live ones, because they are really hard to see until you have practice. The bowl of hot water is where you need to dump whatever you retrieve, and you will dump that into the toilet after you are finished so they don't go hopping onto another kid. If you're like me, you'll gag like crazy during this process. Hang in there!

The most important thing: Send your husband to buy the lice comb. If he grumbles, tell him to grab a dirty magazine while he's at it so if the embarrassment of buying a lice comb bothers him, the promise of wife-approved nudie pic ogling will keep him on task. As for Disney Channel, it may be obnoxious, but it will keep your kid still for six hours straight, and you'll need that time, especially the first time you're navigating the rough waters of this terrible experience. (You are welcome to substitute Disney Channel for the movie *Frozen*, but that alone might push you over the edge.)

The couple's counseling is also hugely necessary, because I'll bet you money that at least 15% of divorces happen because of domestic lice infestations. And the case of red wine is the most obvious item. It will gently soothe you as you handle the immense guilt that comes with realizing you and your family members are dirty, foul sloths who should be ashamed of yourselves for having kids in the first place.

Most importantly, take the time to get your pediatrician to prescribe the heavy duty prescription lice shampoo. I am certain that this glorious mixture is the reason that I am now able to eradicate lice within mere hours. The combination of the heavy-duty shampoo and a good combing will knock those suckers out in half the time of a traditional lice kit. Super earthy moms and dads will disagree with me here, but sometimes, you have to do what you have to do. Now, after I created this survival guide a few years ago, lice removal salons started popping up in my city. Let me tell you, if that's an option, that's the way to go. Do not pass go and head straight to the lice removal salon. (I'd still buy the wine, though).

For those of you who don't have that option, a disclaimer. I wouldn't be able to sleep at night if I didn't warn you about the prescription shampoo. It turns my hands white for hours, so Tim has to do the hair-washing while I watch Disney Channel and drink wine. I read through the possible side effects, and while it's not stated in black and white, it's pretty evident that this shampoo will cause you or your child to grow an extra toe. But the way I look at it, what's an extra toe here or there when you have a lice-free home? Just add a pair of industrial scissors to the Lice Survival Kit, cut out a space on your shoes for an extra toe and keep moving.

You Will See Shrek

From the time Emily Rose was born, she did weird stuff to make us laugh. When she was just weeks old, she had this tripped out thing she would do where her eyes would wander all around and it looked like she was on LSD. It probably should have warranted a call to the pediatrician, but instead, we laughed at it. A lot.

At the time, the classy number, "Hot In Herre" by Nelly was a big hit, so I would sing it to her when I changed her clothes, because to me, there's nothing funnier than singing dirty hip hop songs to babies.

"It's getting hot in here, so take off all your clothes."

I am getting so hot, I wanna take my clothes off."

In other words, it should have been fairly evident to everyone around me that when Emily Rose was born, I lost my ever-loving mind. I wonder often if her sense of humor was a built-in infant coping mechanism designed to help me with my depression, because that baby was hilarious. Before she could speak, she started in on the jokes. I picked her up from daycare one afternoon when she was about six months old, and in the relatively short drive home, she conked out. When we got home, I went back to cautiously unclip her from her carseat, hoping she would stay asleep, and when I touched her to unbuckle the seatbelt, she looked right at me and burst out laughing. Never in my life have I seen a baby play possum. Where did she learn that? I could just kick myself for not taking a video of it.

I've always said that dads connect better with kids once they can talk because I think men prefer verbal feedback. But I actually think it's true for both parents - once Emily Rose started talking, it was a game-changer for all of us. One afternoon I picked her up from daycare and was driving home via our normal route on Lamar Boulevard. We were on a particularly windy stretch near Pease Park where Tim proposed to me (and also where we make out sometimes on date nights and get busted by the cops, but that's supposed to be a secret). I always kept a good view of Emily Rose in the rear view mirror, and as I rounded a corner and looked back, she was missing from view.

"Emily Rose!" I shrieked. "Where are you!?"

"Down here," she said, voice muffled.

She was upside down in the floorboard. I was still driving with no place to pull over, so I kept talking.

"Are you okay?"

"Yes," she said, not at all rattled. "It's kind of weird down here."

Evidently, in my constant state of brain fog of doing my best at being a wife, raising two stepchildren and a baby, I managed to clip Emily Rose into her car seat but failed to check and ensure that the car seat itself was clipped onto the seat. I pulled the car over, ran around to the back seat and yanked her out of the floorboard, and once I realized she was fine, we laughed our heads off.

It got even more fun when Emily Rose got old enough to draw and invent things. She invented, "Cleodorant," a deodorant for cleavage. She didn't understand why people put deodorant on their underarms but ignore their cleavage, which she contends is equally as sweaty as armpits. She carefully removed the label from a container of deodorant and painted a homemade label, then promptly made up a jingle for it. We thought briefly about pitching it on *Shark Tank* since it seemed like a pretty fabulous idea.

When Emily Rose was in preschool, Tim and I were both working crazy hours, so we spent a lot of family dinners in restaurants. At the time, we ate at a neighborhood Chinese restaurant pretty regularly because we could bribe the kids with edamame and chicken and rice, but Emily Rose was mainly interested in the fortune cookies. One night after we finished dinner, we were opening up our fortune cookies and reading them out loud. Emily Rose was about three and wasn't yet reading, but she opened up her fortune cookie and after we read ours, looked at hers and said, "You will see *Shrek*."

It took a minute for this to sink in, but once Tim and I realized that Emily Rose was using a fortune cookie to manipulate us into letting her watch her favorite movie that night, we realized that this kid was going to keep us on our toes. This was around the same time that Emily Rose suddenly had a new hairstyle, and refused to admit to us or the preschool teacher that she was cutting her own hair. She refused so vehemently that at one point, I actually believed her, even though the teacher kept showing us chunks of hair that were randomly showing up in the classroom books. I'm telling you, the kid was GOOD.

When Emily Rose had just turned 10, Tim and I took her to San Francisco. Ten is a cool age, because that's when you're really starting to observe what's happening around you and where you start deciding for yourself what is right and wrong. One evening after a long day touring the city, we stopped at a very popular sushi restaurant by our hotel that was known for having a terrifically diverse crowd, including lots of transgender diners. Lucky for us, this wasn't shocking for Emily Rose because we live in Austin where transgender diners are as common as software engineers. There was a long wait, and we stood in the crowded bar area near two young men sitting at the bar telling stories. Every other word was "fuck." I'm okay with more than an occasional f-bomb, and I'll be the first to admit I use the word liberally driving in Austin traffic. However, I have some strong opinions about people cussing in front of kids. Evidently, so does Emily Rose.

She kept giving us a sideways glance and nodding over to the guys, and leaning in and saying, "They are cussing *SO MUCH*." The longer we stood there listening, the more annoyed we became. Their vocabulary was like, so fucking limited.

"I want to say something to them." Emily Rose said.

"Okay," Tim said. "If you said something to them, what would you say?"

The brainstorming began. If you had witnessed it, it was a lot like a political team coming up with the right statement for a candidate. It needed to be firm, but also compelling and make a solid point. We pondered a hundred different remarks, and settled on a statement that we all agreed would be highly effective.

We made a plan to execute. Emily Rose would approach the young men and say her piece, and Tim would be near enough if things got weird so he could protect her. I would be near enough on the other side to go Mama Bear if need be, but this was going to be her moment, and because we are such oddball parents, we completely encouraged it as long as she felt comfortable. I took her to the bathroom so she could practice. There was a lot of nervous laughter and excitement as her face flushed red and she said,

"I don't think I can do it! But I really want to! I really want to do this!"

She practiced and practiced. I taught her about Harvard Professor Amy Cuddy and her Ted Talk on the Power Pose, and she posed and posed and practiced her statement until she was ready. By this time, we had a table, but the guys remained in earshot, f-bombing away. We finished dinner, and it was go-time. Tim stood at the steps by the door, and I stayed at the table so we had her covered from both directions, just in case. We watched as she walked up, and we knew exactly what was she was saying.

"Excuse me, but I need to tell you something," she said, hand on her hip. "When you say 'fuck' around a 10 year-old, it makes you seem like a real asshole."

And with that, she walked away as the guys sat there open-mouthed.

We went outside and stood on the slanted San Francisco sidewalk and jumped up and down, high-fiving and laughing all the way to the hotel. It was one of my life's most exhilarating moments. Emily Rose's courage was to be celebrated!

Years later some wet blanket researcher tried to debunk Amy Cuddy's research on the effectiveness of the Power Pose, but I'm here to tell you that the Power Pose worked magically for Emily Rose. When we arrived back at our hotel, exhausted with laughter, we plopped down in the hotel lobby chairs while Emily Rose rocked a perfect Power Pose.

I knew that night that Emily Rose was going to make it in the world, and that she had what she needed to stand up against things she thinks are wrong in the world. She has the power.

Nursing the Sleepover Hangover

When your kid is invited to a sleepover, it's like a commercial for a Royal Caribbean cruise. The list of perks is so sexy, you'd be crazy to deny them. After minimal prep that includes begging your child for the very last time to please put down the hula hoop and pack an overnight bag while your husband makes a beeline for the garage to grab a musty sleeping bag, you're rewarded with the delightful benefits of an easy 14-16 hour break from reality. As you drop off your squealing kid to the kind, unwitting hosts, you leave waving and smiling, knowing in a matter of minutes you and your husband will bask in the glory of a table for two that excludes Crayons, pink lemonade, and a wiggly kid.

At home, you giddily unlock the parental control on Netflix for back-to-back episodes of *Orange is the New Black* because you're always several years behind everyone else on the shows. Your husband, warmed up by the full frontal nudity, pours you another glass of wine and offers you a back rub. Thank you, sleepovers!

You rise glowing and rested, noting that it's so quiet that you can imagine your life together as retired people. You take one look at your husband when you realize you're the retired people on the Viagra commercial. Your passion reignited, instead of sneaking in a muffled Saturday morning quickie before the kids wake up, you take full advantage of having the green light to engage in the kind of passion that's normally reserved for hotels and Kardashians. You spend the rest of the morning drinking coffee and reading the newspaper, refreshed and ready to conquer the weekend.

Then you pick up your kid.

The happy, pumped-up ball of energy you dropped off last night has been replaced by a child you hardly recognize. The kid who hugged you tightly and thanked you endlessly for allowing you to spend a night away from home greets you with a blank stare that would worry Putin. With effort, you manage to get your kid to thank the host for inviting them when you realize that the host is also greeting you with the same blank gaze. You are afraid. You scan the floor for wayward socks, grab the unfolded sleeping bag and haul ass to the SUV before things get ugly.

That's when it hits you. Your kid has a sleepover hangover.

You've been here before, but parental amnesia is part of the package, so naturally you didn't see it coming. It's a lot like your cousin Sal's wedding. Remember that lusty trifecta of wedding romance with Sal's college roommate, an open bar and an '80s cover band? When you woke the next morning in an unfamiliar hotel room wearing Sal's roommate's bow tie and little else, reversing the decisions from the night before wasn't exactly an option.

When you guide your zombie-like child into the car, you

must minimize conversation. Otherwise, someone is bound to say something regrettable. Don't bother asking the kid what time they went to sleep because you don't want to know the answer. The car ride home will likely lull your child back to sleep, so depending on their age and weight, you'll probably want to ask your husband to carry them inside. He'll be rejuvenated from your morning tryst, so he'll happily oblige.

Here's the easy part: sleepover hangovers are just like regular hangovers. It's all about rest and rehydration. Even better, unless the kid completely binged on pizza and Sour Patch Straws, it's unlikely that they'll spend the morning puking. Gently guide the kid into their bed or onto the couch, hydrate them with orange juice and feed them a super carby-breakfast. Turn on cartoons, a fan, and turn out the lights. I usually stick around to make sure the kid doesn't pass out in the middle of eating a toaster strudel, just to be safe.

Just like a regular hangover, you'll want to wake the kid every few hours and give them more liquids. Wash, rinse, repeat until the child looks like your child again, and only then should you inform them that they will never attend another sleepover again. At least not for a few more weekends.

Piggy Piggy Confessions

I'll be the first to admit I have a list of pet peeves a mile long, but one of my biggest pet peeves is piggy piggyness. The term "piggy piggy" has been thrown around my house for years, and has several meanings. For example, you know when you get up in the middle of the night and are so ravenous you can't wait until daylight, so you creep into the kitchen and eat something you'd feel ashamed to eat any other time? Those late night snack sneaks are what we call "piggy piggy confessions."

We all have something that we're piggy piggy about. I happen to know a wonderful, otherwise self-disciplined lady who sneaks a few sexy spoonfuls of cake icing in the middle of the night. I know another who gets up and serves herself a "cocktail" of pickle juice on ice with a cold pickle garnish. I also happen to know a mother of three who gets up in the middle of the night and eats messy little handfuls of imitation bacon bits, because I am that woman.

The word can take on a few meanings. For the purpose of today's lesson here is how I define piggy piggy:

> **piggy piggy: adjective, verb, adverb, you name it: 1. the overwhelming desire to grab**

**something that's free. 2. the state of being con-
sumed by the need to be the first to obtain
an object, free or otherwise.** *That piggy piggy
girl skipped in the school lunch line to get the
last chocolate milk. She piggy piggied herself
in front of three cars to get that parking spot.
At last night's free concert in the park, a family
piggy piggily put their lawn chairs in front of
us and blocked our view of REO Speedwagon!*

When I lived in LA in my 20s, I worked for a magazine that sponsored a charity 5K with Revlon, and before the race began, the participants were invited to come to a tent where the sponsors would give away everything from branded stress balls to tiny bottles of nail polish to coupons. My company decided that instead of cheap plastic junk, we would give away apples. Plain Jane, grocery store, pesticide-sprayed apples. But by the way those women pushed and pulled to get to free apples, you would think we were giving away apples dipped in gold. I had to yell at the top of my lungs, "Ladies, ladies! These are *apples*! Please stop pushing!"

I'm sure there's some kind of psychological condition that explains why people lose all sense of dignity in a sudden race for free things, but that was the first time I'd seen it in action on such a grand scale, and it both upset me and grossed me out at the same time. The Free Apple Incident coined the word piggy piggy. And I've been running into piggy piggy moments ever since.

Society really encourages piggypiggyness. It's the "first come, first served" mentality we've all grown up with that makes us feel that we need to fight for what we feel we deserve. And for people like my grandparents who grew up during The Depression, free apples might have induced some serious excitement, but that's because they were hungry and had hungry relatives to help feed. But this is not about *true* hunger, it's about the competition that's born from greed.

You could own three bottom drawers full of ugly printed t-shirts that are being used as car towels, but go to a sports event where they start shooting t-shirts out of a t-shirt gun, and you'll run over an elderly man with an oxygen tank to claim a free shirt you'll never wear because it's too small. And do you want to know why that shirt is too small? Because you're the same guy who shoves his way in front of others to eat the free guacamole and stale chip samples at the grocery store. It's about winning. But what are you winning?

Think about how we behave in traffic, and how many people feel completely at ease with pulling over into the right lane and speeding past hundreds of people who were being patient enough to wait their turn. It's piggy piggy. Think about grocery store lines, and how people will pretend not to see you and race you to the checkout. I once saw an entire news segment on how to best game the system so you can piggy piggy yourself in front at the grocery.

When the kids were little I constantly reminded them not to go after the last piece of bread in the bread basket without asking if anyone else would like it first. And now, thankfully, my kids actually ask if someone wants the last piece of bread before taking it. I'm expecting this to transfer outside of my home, so that when my kids have dinner with other families, the parents will be stupefied by my children's manners. Tim, one of the least piggy piggy people I know, leads by example, and shows our kids that you should open doors and let people go in front of you. I'm really not trying to be one of those "In OUR family we" kind of people because those memes are so braggy pants it makes me gag. Nevertheless, we know our kids face competition on a daily basis, so we try to instill that life is not always about being first and winning, but enjoying what it feels like to step back and have a little grace. Hopefully, when my kids have kids, they will teach my grandchildren not to be piggy piggy. And hopefully, this expression will go viral and become part of our modern-day lexicon, because I'm pretty certain that Emily Rose thinks that piggy piggy is an actual commonly-used phrase.

Please don't let me make you think I'm perfect in this area, because I'm absolutely not. One afternoon my coworker and I were walking back to our office after grabbing coffee, and we passed a friendly hippie selling organic fruits and veggies outside a little restaurant. He had fresh peaches, and held one in his hand and offered it to my friend, and said, "Take it. It's free!"

As my coworker, a close friend whom I adore, took the peach into her hand, I felt a sudden primal urge to knock her to the ground to get a peach of my own. I wanted one of those peaches, and I wanted it to be free! But I thought better of it, not because a lady never succumbs to her piggy piggy urges, but because I don't eat hairy foods.

So perhaps I shouldn't worry about passing any wisdom along to others until I've learned to control my own piggy piggy desires. But if I pass the hippie fruit and veggie vendor and he's passing out imitation bacon bits, stay the hell out of my way.

Jesus Was a Hipster

I've always said I've had an on-again, off-again relationship with Jesus. It started with growing up Methodist, where in my view, being religious and being a Methodist meant that you did nice things for other people and you were part of a really supportive, loving community of people who would show up with a casserole when things got rough. Being a Methodist meant you knew all the words to the Doxology, you went to some kind of retreat or camp a few times a year, and during the hymns, you could sing the alto line without hesitation. I liked all of that.

The Methodist church where I spent most of my youth didn't push Jesus on you too much. You knew he was a good guy who wasn't judgy and was kind to poor people. I always figured if Jesus did come back around in my lifetime, he'd be the kind of guy we all wanted to hang out with. Yet, I struggled with grasping the concept of Jesus just showing up unannounced and everyone believing it.

Since my religious upbringing was extremely positive for the most part, I knew that when I started a family I wanted my kids to at least have a religious foundation so they could discover their own ideas about life and God. After I married Tim, I converted to Catholicism because it was really important to me that Emily Rose and I had the same religious foundation as Tim and the kids. While none of us were particularly gung-ho about going to church, I signed up to help create a tighter bond with the family. But I should rephrase that. You don't just "sign up" to become Catholic. They totally make you work at it. You spend nearly an entire year preparing to convert, which I thought was so weird given that Methodists and Catholics share so many similarities. I kind of thought I would place out of most of the program, but the Catholics don't exactly allow you to cut corners.

When Tim and I first started talking about my conversion, and Tim said, "It really is pretty much the same, except we believe the blood is really blood and the body is really body."

That was totally weird to me, and I didn't want to think about being a vampire or a cannibal, so I tried to focus on the other stuff.

The first step was a meeting with the priest, and in that sense, I totally scored in the priest department. Our guy was a large, funny, former Southern Baptist who also converted to become a Catholic and then he got so gung-ho about it he became a priest. That was a plus for me because he was already very accepting and open. I decided the best way to talk about conversion with a priest is to hit the big ticket items right off the bat. I also decided that honesty was the best policy since after all, I was talking to a man of God.

"Look," I said, as we sat casually in a stuffy incense-smelling church office one afternoon, "I'm all about signing on to do this, especially given that I grew up Methodist, so we're basically on the same page except for a few details. Still, I need you to know that I disagree with at least five of the big things you guys believe in."

He sat calmly with his arms crossed, listening.

"For starters, I think you need women in the clergy. You're hurting for priests as it is, and women are just as good at it if not better. No offense."

"None taken," he said, a little tickled at my candor.

"I think your ideas about birth control are outdated and dangerous. Why should we encourage unwanted pregnancies when we have too many unwanted children to care for as it is?"

He kept listening.

"I am Pro Choice. I always will be. I am okay with being against the death penalty, though. I know it seems like a contradiction but I believe a woman should be able to have an abortion if she chooses to do that. I'm against the death penalty because I think we get it wrong too often and that, to me, is not our call."

"Mmm."

"And I totally don't understand the church's stance on homosexuality given that most of you guys are gayer than Clay Aiken."

The priest laughed. He really liked me — or he really liked Clay Aiken. (He was kind of a big deal at the time.)

"Do you believe in justice?" he asked.

"Sure."

"Do you believe in caring for the poor and the vulnerable?"

"Totally."

"Do you believe in the teachings of Jesus?"

"Yes, I really think Jesus was a good guy."

"Well, the things you are talking about are 'political things,'" he said. "These are things that you can work out with Jesus in time."

I wasn't really satisfied with that answer, because of my on again, off again relationship with Jesus. Part of this was that talking to Jesus was always very awkward to me, and it took me back to the seventh grade when I felt forced to have a conversation with him.

In middle school, a lot of my friends went to a "non denominational" camp in East Texas that would be better named "Jesus Camp." A heads up in case you aren't aware: every summer camp in East Texas is Jesus camp. At Jesus Camp, from the first day, the counselors and staff started pressuring me to ask Jesus to be my "personal Lord and savior." It was basically the main goal of the camp. If you ask me, that's a pretty daunting question for a pre-teen. I was just trying to figure out ropes courses and waterskiing.

Camp was so much fun, but the pressure to get right with Jesus weighed heavily on me. Like everything important, I procrastinated. Kids around me were getting "saved" left and right, but I just didn't feel ready.

Finally, on the last night of camp, I found a quiet spot on a bench in the piney woods of East Texas and gave it a shot.

"Hey, Jesus, I know you've been getting a lot of this lately, but I need to ask you something. Would you be interested in being my personal Lord and savior?" I recall that I asked it like I was ordering a personal pizza. "And, um, could I like, have eternal life with that? And maybe a side of peppercorn ranch?"

"Um, Jesus?"

He never replied back, so I just assumed his answer was no.

So when the priest suggested that I take up the political items with Jesus, that pressure to do things perfectly came back again. Still, I'm a pretty obedient type despite my need to ask rebellious questions, and I truly try to follow instructions, so at the priest's suggestion, I decided to work it out with Jesus as soon as possible. I started walking around Austin, looking around for him. The problem in Austin is that more than half of the guys here look JUST LIKE JESUS! Everywhere you turn, it's a guy with long hair, a beard, and sandals. But if you think about it, you know that Jesus was just a big old hipster, even way back then. Lucky for the guys in Austin, I haven't had the courage to stop someone who looks like Jesus and say,

"Pardon me, man, but could we sit down on a rock and discuss your feelings about condoms? I also need to work out abortion and homosexuality if you have a few minutes."

So far, I haven't worked these things out and I haven't changed my mind, but I can't help but think that since Jesus hung out with prostitutes and gamblers and otherwise unsavory characters, deep down, he would be okay. Hipsters are cool like that.

The Casserole Network

sk anyone who has an affiliation with a religious organization, no matter the flavor, and they will tell you that when a baby is born, someone has surgery, or someone dies, the women in their community come together and cook meals to take to the families in need. Even for the non-religious, when someone is in need, women coordinate to cook and deliver food. It's just what you do.

Since my mother and grandmothers on both sides were Methodist women, as far as I knew, life's big dramatic events meant something fully unrecognizable and ridiculously delicious would arrive at your home. And almost every time, it would come in a Pyrex dish covered with aluminum foil. In Texas, this means that your pantry must always include a back-up supply of cream of mushroom soup, and you can never have enough aluminum foil. I'm not sure if the cream of mushroom craze is universal. In remote Alaska, their version of The Casserole Network might be cream of elk's feet.

This network is magic to me. I'm sure you can trace the origins to before telephones were invented, when carrier pigeons shared the news of an illness or death, and from there, women made large vats of soup to help their friends in need. Today, there are numerous online meal sign-up platforms to make it really easy to coordinate.

My friend Amy is in a league of her own when it comes to meal delivery. She's a pro, sending emails or texts and getting the job done while the rest of us are contemplating gift cards. Amy can plan a baby shower in less than 15 minutes, down to beautiful personalized napkins. She's also the friend who announced boldly before having children that she would *never* serve frozen lasagna to dinner guests in her home. We teased her relentlessly about this, but two children later, I think she's actually sticking to her word. Meanwhile, if Queen Elizabeth came to visit unannounced, I'd probably whip out a frozen lasagna and call it a day, but that's just me.

I have always believed that The Casserole Network is more like the scene in *Snow White* where Snow White bakes a pie with the assistance of animated birds with culinary experience. I like to think that when someone gets sick, a vast network of animated church ladies simultaneously begin whipping up casseroles while animated birds pull processed cheese out of the fridge. There's some whistling. It's wholesome and pure. In this world, nobody cusses like a truck driver like I did when I burned my arm making pasticcio for Geography Day when Stephanie was in elementary school. I should have just brought napkins.

A few years ago, my mom had foot surgery, and the network kicked in right away. At the time, my parents lived in a wonderful little house in my hometown of Tyler, Texas. The house had some definite quirks. For one, it was designed by a creative architect who may have had a little drug problem, or had some hatred for the elderly or temporarily disabled. Each room in the home was on a different level, so in order to get from one room to the next, you confronted some stairs. The rooms were small, and the floor plan wound itself up from the ground floor for a total of seven unique little levels to a balcony outside of the top bedroom. The home was basically an indoor Swiss Family Treehouse, except my parents didn't sleep in hammocks, and they didn't pass down dirty dishes on dumbwaiters made out of rope and sticks. But otherwise, the climbing was about the same.

When my mother, a very strong-willed and independent type, called to tell me she was having foot surgery, I wasn't surprised when she said she wouldn't need my help. But I got to thinking about the quirky house with the stairs, and started imagining my mother toppling down the stairs in her black Velcro boot, while my stepfather the artist was drawing in his studio several rooms below, completely unaware. I decided I needed to be there to help out, and that was that.

I arrived at the Swiss Family Treehouse the evening before the surgery to determine my duties and rest up for my mother's surgery day. While catching up, my mother told me that several weeks ago, one of her dearest friends had a neck injury that required surgery. Because she's a prominent member of the Casserole Network, my mother and other Sunday school friends arranged a dinner delivery, each taking on a portion of the meal. The woman who volunteered for dessert is a woman after my own heart. She started with grand illusions of making a homemade dessert, but life got in the way, and her backup plan was to buy ice cream. I could just hug her neck for that. My mother offered to handle the delivery, and, because of logistics, planned to meet the dessert volunteer at a local convenience store parking lot.

So far I've been pretty sexist here, failing to mention how men fit into this delicate picture. But let's call a spade a spade, because we all know that most men don't go whipping up chicken taco casseroles when their friends get sick. I've heard of exceptions, and in fact married a man who carves watermelons into baskets to host his intricate fruit salads, but for today's story let's consider that women are running this business and the menfolk get to carry the hot plates.

On this particular afternoon, my mother and stepfather were in a convenience store parking lot, waiting on the dessert volunteer. It was about 127 degrees, a typical late Texas summer afternoon. My mother does most of the driving, so my stepfather was in the passenger seat with a piping hot Pyrex dish of chicken spaghetti casserole on his lap. He was loving life, I'm sure. He's a skinny man in his 80s who has taken to wearing baseball caps with messages on them. If you had told me 30 years ago that he would be wearing baseball caps, I would fall on the floor laughing. Yet somehow these hats suit him now. The hat he wears the most sports the famous Davy Crockett quote, "You may all go to Hell, and I will go to Texas." In other words, cross this man in a convenience store parking lot, and he might just toss a hot casserole at you.

The scene was looking pretty suspicious as my parents waited on the dessert volunteer. Evidently the dessert volunteer was a woman my mom didn't know well so she wasn't sure how she would spot her. Since my mother also does most of the talking, she turned to my stepfather, and said, "How are we going to know which car is hers?"

My stepfather, in his typical deadpan style, said, "She'll be driving the car with ice cream dripping out of the car doors."

Soon enough, the dessert volunteer arrived and she and my mother made a shady-looking exchange with a plastic bag filled with individual ice creams in a variety of excellent flavors, thankfully still frozen. The patient and her husband were delighted; The Casserole Network's job was done.

Just a few weeks later, it was my mother's turn to be the patient. As a bossy firstborn daughter who appears to be "in charge," I learned that I was not mentally prepared to be my mother's caretaker. She's too strong and independent. She's really good at getting things done. At the end of the day, I'm a big spoiled baby who likes to see my mom up and at it when I'm at her house. But because my sister had fallen ill several days before and would typically be with me to help out, I ended up being the person in charge. My stepfather, also not fired up at the idea of my mother being partially immobile for six weeks, graciously allowed me to enter the treehouse and take over.

Given the circumstances, I cannot stress how lifesaving the Casserole Network is at times like this. Even before my mother's surgery, the network's machine was smoothly running in the background, waiting for go time. As my mother recovered, the home phone would ring and a friend would be on the line, offering up delivery times that worked best for our schedules. It was a huge help.

I recently had the honor of being on the giving side of the Casserole Network when a friend's mother was hospitalized. The hardest part of receiving help is asking for it, but my friend swallowed his pride and simply posted this on Facebook:

"Friends, I am overwhelmed. I need help with food preparation and delivery."

He then added that he hated asking for help, but the network refused to let him apologize, and thanked him for having the guts to come out and ask. The Network kicked in gear right away. Men and women signed up to bring meals, drop off gift cards, and whip up casseroles. I was delighted to be able to sign up for meal prep online, making a note:

"I was raised Methodist. I was born for this!"

Several days later, we had a parking lot handoff where I proudly handed over a chicken taco casserole made primarily of cream of chicken soup and Velveeta, with a bagged salad for a semblance of nutritional balance.

No matter how hard it is for us to accept help, there comes a time when we all need it, and there is nothing better than a Pyrex dish covered in foil, a Tupperware bowl of fresh salad, and a Ziploc bag of cookies to ease the patient and their family down the road to recovery.

Also Allergic to Crafting

When my sister Emily got engaged, we all knew her wedding would be one for the record books. The wedding theme was vintage circus, which was very cool because my sister and her fiancé Rocky are both extremely creative people who love all things vintage. They had a massive guest list and a ton of DIY projects to complete, ensuring that their wedding would truly be "The Other Greatest Show on Earth." My sister sweetly asked me to be her Maid of Honor, and of course, I accepted under one condition. Since the proper title is "matron," I refused to be referred to as matron of anything. I would be called a Maid of Honor. It's very fitting as I am extremely youthful and maidenesque.

One of the challenges in being a Maid of Honor is you risk being asked to do DIY projects, and since I can hardly make cookies from the packages of pre-made dough without catching something on fire, when my sister sent a pre-wedding email with instructions for the bridesmaids to wear vintage headpieces, I hoped to God I would find a reasonably priced one online. However, I'm a terrible combination of not being crafty and waiting until the last minute to buy things for costume parties, and since her wedding was the most important costume party of our lives, I waited until the last minute and completely freaked out when I realized I'd have to make my own headpiece.

I hate crafts and craft stores with equal passion. When my kids were little and came home with turkeys made out of traced hands glued onto popsicle sticks, I had to fake appreciation before hiding them in keepsake bins under the bed. While the other PTA moms were racing each other to the craft store to make pilgrims out of cotton balls and pipe cleaners, I would just send Tim to the store to pick up juice boxes while I drank wine and watched *The Real Housewives of NYC.*

Just mere days before the wedding, I ventured out to two of the most anxiety-provoking establishments known to non-crafty types: Jo-Ann Fabrics and Hobby Lobby. For me, the only thing worse is a trip to Pep Boys. Stop #1 was Jo-Ann, where I set out to locate fuschia feathers, some kind of pearl/rhinestone embellishment, and a stretchy headband. I started by looking for an employee to ask for guidance, but since stores don't really have those anymore, I grabbed a cart and wandered over to the faux flower section. I meandered through every aisle, grabbing anything that resembled a feather and tossing it into the cart while I groaned audibly and rolled my eyes at the overhead cameras. Like anyone would steal this shit!

I learned a lot during that journey. Like, for example, there are so many kinds of jewelry clasps in this world, they take up *an entire aisle* of real estate at Jo-Ann. I learned that where artificial flowers are concerned, they're a lot like eyelash extensions - despite a lot of effort to make them look real, 90% of them look totally fake. I also learned that the person responsible for the music played in Jo-Ann stores very possibly spent their previous career torturing prisoners at Gitmo.

Overwhelmed, I followed the maze of monogrammed plastic drink cups and patriotic flip-flops and made my way to the button aisle, hoping to find a vintage-looking buttony thing to glue onto the headband. The button aisle borders the area where people willingly look at pattern books. I spotted a customer there, sitting in front of a 1987 desktop computer, talking on the phone. She was a sweet-faced woman wearing a bright purple sweatshirt with a bedazzled cross on it.

"I thought I'd add some lace to the bottom of it," she said happily. Her cheeks were flushed with excitement at the mere mention of her creative process. "Oh yes, honey, I'm at Jo-Ann. I'll be here all morning!"

Aghast, I made my way to the check-out. A teenager in a smock stood by the only open register. She was talking to another smocked teen who was pretending to sweep the floor while they chatted. I put my fuchsia feathers on the counter while I waited for her to greet me.

"I should have called in," the teen at the register said to the teen with the broom, ignoring me completely.

"You need Emergen-C," said the teen with the broom while I stepped back and began holding my breath.

"No, I'm pretty sure it's strep," she said, coughing into her hand, then using the same hand to swipe my feathers over the scanner. "I've had a fever for, like, three days."

I thought briefly about asking to speak with the

manager—partly because the kid spent more time talking to her coworker than addressing her extremely reluctant customer, but mainly because she came to work with SARS and that's just rude. But I was already weary, so I used my elbows to pick up the feathers, and while heading to the car, it dawned on me that one of those poor girls was more than likely the manager anyway. It was all so very sad.

Stop #2 was Hobby Lobby. Forgive me Father, for I have sinned. I swore after Hobby Lobby's shenanigans about birth control that I would never set foot inside a Hobby Lobby again (not that I set foot in there many times anyway), but desperate times call for desperate measures. As I approached the door, I checked out the clientele going inside. Walking up on my right was another woman with a bedazzled cross on her chest. Par for the course. Walking up to my left? A woman with a Bernie Sanders t-shirt and a sheepish expression of guilt. That made me laugh. Knowing we were all in it together, I entered the store, prepared for the worst.

A woman with overdyed red hair and lipstick-smeared teeth pointed me in the direction of the stretchy headbands and feathers, and I grabbed up more supplies and headed for the checkout. The median age of the cashiers working at Hobby Lobby that particular morning was around 93. For a company that has a moral objection to birth control, I find it deliciously ironic that the women working at Hobby Lobby haven't needed birth control for at least five decades. Guilt-ridden from spending $6.17 at a store that I promised not to patronize (or, more fittingly, matronize), I headed home with two bags of craft supplies, fully spent.

Several days later I mustered up the courage to start the project, but not before I invited Michelle, one of the more crafty bridesmaids, to come over and help. We were equipped with the necessary supplies: a stack of craft nonsense and two bottles of champagne. We're smart ladies.

I love how several glasses of bubbly can give you the required confidence to navigate a corporate happy hour, dance in public, or make vintage headpieces. With Michelle's delightful company, I managed to survive hot-gluing feathers onto stretchy headbands, and within a little over an hour, we were finished. My biggest fear was that I would glue my fingers together with E 6000 craft glue, or that my headpiece would make me look like a retired prostitute. However, thanks to Michelle's help and focus, we whipped out two quality products. They were so good that we talked about selling them afterward to another set of frazzled bridesmaids, but I think I'll save mine to pass down to one of my daughters to prove that, at one point in time, their mom actually crafted.

Welcome to Vietnam

When I married Tim, I married a hoarder.

Tim's is a special case, though, and not something that should cause you to worry for my family's safety. Before you conjure up the images from TV's sad but addictive "Hoarders," we don't live in a home with stacks of empty pizza boxes, and you don't have to shove your way through piles of clothes or newspapers to get into any of our rooms. Sure, we have our messes, but most of the inside of our house is passable and pretty normal. However, if you come to our house, you may find that the blinds that cover our back kitchen window will be lowered and closed, because there are times when that action is a necessity. It's about hiding the backyard and the garage area. I'll try to explain.

My sister has my favorite way of describing Tim's particularly variety of hoarding:

"When the Revolution comes, I'm going to live with Tim."

That's because when the Revolution comes, we may not have extra cases of canned goods and bottled water, and we don't have guns, but one thing is certain: we more than likely have one or two of whatever else you might need if the world is coming to an end.

Tim has a few things that he is passionate about. He loves politics and being a Texas Democrat. He loves helping people. He loves fixing things. And he loves finding bargains. He is happiest when he's digging through things at a garage sale or thrift store. Sometimes, I enjoy going with him. I love to look across a room and see Tim, wearing a pair of reading glasses, carefully inspecting something. You can almost see a thought bubble above his head where his brain is processing what he's going to do with whatever random object he's inspecting.

One of Tim's favorite places to find things is the Goodwill Outlet. The Goodwill Outlet sells items that have been through the ultimate rejection: they are not even good enough for Goodwill. Tim sees this as his own personal Island of Lost Toys. Tim has had such an intimate relationship the Goodwill Outlet than he lovingly calls it "BH" after their former name, "Blue Hanger."

When it comes to clothing and household goods, there is a definite hierarchy, and it goes like this:

The Actual Retail Store. It could be Nordstrom or Old Navy, but at some point, things start out new.

High End Consignment Shops - These shops offer high end, gently loved clothing, and the owner makes a portion of the sale after the item is purchased.

Family/Friend Handoffs - If it's good enough, you'll save items for your friends and give them away so they stay near and dear. My sister and her friends refer to this as "keeping it in the family."

Goodwill or Your Best Local Charity: Things that don't

pass the Family and Friend Handoff test end up bagged up and given to Goodwill.

The Goodwill Outlet - When Goodwill doesn't want it, it goes to BH.

The Dumpster - When BH doesn't want it, I'm fairly sure it ends up in a dumpster.

A Landfill. From there, it dies a slow death.

I find it necessary to lay this groundwork so you can understand what kind of stuff my husband enjoys digging through, because in these piles, he finds some really remarkable things. The best example is that twice, Tim has found a Mont Blanc pen in the stacks of crap at BH. That kind of find keeps Tim high on life for weeks on end. But it's worth stating in order to find Mont Blanc pens at BH, Tim made a conscious decision to dig through piles that are just one step above dumpsters. And Tim Arndt is certainly not above digging in a dumpster, especially if it's at the end of the semester and the students at The University of Texas have just moved out.

Allow me to set the scene for you so you can understand what "BH" is all about. BH is a huge warm and somewhat smelly warehouse full of long tables that are fashioned into long bins to store all of the stuff that the employees pile in there. There is a definite set of rules about how this all goes down. The tables are emptied on a regular basis, and then the employees haul out huge blue bins of "new" merchandise, and they dump them in one long row of tables. While this goes on, the shoppers must stand behind a line before they are allowed to go through the merchandise.

Talk about Piggy Piggy. There is something very disturbing

about watching this scene go down. When the "new" stuff is placed and ripe for the picking, one of the employees makes a "go" motion and then otherwise normal humans clobber one another to dig into piles of crap that nobody wants at Goodwill. When this happens, I guess Tim gets some kind of Dopamine-induced thrill. I hate it. I choose not to participate in the digging around of the new stuff, because I have serious personal space issues and getting in the middle of that nonsense is like being in a subway in New York at rush hour, only everyone is grabbing and throwing used merchandise around. Instead, I choose to look around at the stuff that's already been picked over on an aisle far away from the mayhem.

I have one steadfast rule when I go with Tim to BH. As soon as I touch something wet, I'm out of there. But, aside from the soft embrace of my loving arms, this is truly Tim's happy place. Actually, my loving arms are probably his second choice if he had to decide. The guy really likes his BH.

Because of all of the collecting, when someone needs something, and they ask Tim, his typical response is this:

"What color do you need?" Then he laughs his huge gigantic Bert laugh and heads back to the garage.

For a few years we had a Syrian neighbor named George. George was a sculptor, and most of the time when you saw George, he was filthy because he was working on something phenomenal in his little garage apartment studio down the road. He would come out of his garage apartment only to discuss his project or ask for supplies. I'm pretty sure when George was working on a project, he didn't come out of his garage to eat. The man was bone skinny. Whenever George needed supplies, he knew to come to our house, because Tim could hook him up. One day, George knocked on the door.

"Is Tim home?" George asked, breathless and excited.

"Yep, he's out in the back," I said. "Enter at your own risk." I make jokes to cover the pain.

About that time, Tim emerged, about as filthy as George.

"Tim, I need a football."

"What color?" Tim asked.

"I also need a lasso."

Tim darted off to the garage and returned with an actual lasso and a football. Also, it should be worth noting that it didn't take him three days to find it. Tim's particular variety of hoarding usually means that he can find what you need in a matter of minutes.

Not that the year's worth of stuff is catalogued in any form or fashion. As you walk down our back steps and into the garage area, you may trip over an antique chair that needs repair. You may notice a pile of life vests, or a set of snow skis. Perhaps you need a set of chili pepper string lights? Tim has them. In green. And red.

Tim takes great pleasure in finding something, paying little to nothing for it, cleaning it up and repurposing it. Usually, when he repurposes something, he is helping someone else. He's not exactly religious, but I consider Tim's hoarding to be his own little ministry. He has helped deck out several apartments for people in need, including a man who was homeless for 40 years and when he finally got an apartment, Tim delivered him chairs so when his case worker came to visit, they had a nice place to sit. I can poke fun of this man for hoarding up BH and dumpster finds all I want, but at the end of the day, I married a saint.

I have a friend who feels very strongly that books have souls. I believe that Tim sees some kind of almost living and breathing value in stuff. He often tells me that he buys something at a garage sale, estate sale, or one of the Goodwill reject stores because he feels that whatever he brings home will be part of a greater project. He'll buy the vintage wooden oars because we may get a canoe again and then we'll already have oars. He'll buy the little piece that fixes the 8-track because someday, we may have an 8-track again (which is actually true, since Tim also bought a dilapidated boat that has an 8-track player. See? It all comes together).

Want more examples? There are so, so many:

- My sister Emily used to help plan Halloween events for an Austin band that held an annual bash with different themes. One year, Tim found a casket on the side of the road, and he loaded it up to give to Emily. Said casket remained a part of Emily's life for many years. Yep, a CASKET.

- We hosted a group of Danish students who visited Austin during the fall for a study abroad. On Halloween night, close to 20 Danish kids spent their evening out on Austin's 6th Street, dressed head to toe in costumes that Tim provided.

- A new neighbor moved in across the street to attend grad school at UT, and when Tim went over to introduce himself, realized the kid didn't have much in the way of furniture, so within minutes, he came out with chairs for the living room and front porch, and one of those portable gazebo things for his patio. Voila!

- Years before Uber was created, my girlfriend had a birthday and we wanted to take her to a restaurant and vineyard about an hour out of town. Tim volunteered to be our chauffeur for the night. He fashioned a curtain out of material he had in the garage, and of course he also wore a black driver's hat (the captain variety) that he gifted to a little kid when he came to pick us up. The hat served its purpose; time to move on to a new owner who would enjoy it even more than Tim did. (It should go without saying that Tim doesn't abide by the Never Wear Anyone Else's Hat rule in the least).

This is the man I married. Perhaps you're starting to get the idea. For the examples above and then some and some and some and some more, and for the mere fact that the entire time I've been married to Tim, our life has included a LOT of stuff, years ago, my sister aptly named our situation Vietnam. For starters, our garage area looks very much like a war zone. It's also a war zone that appears to have no end in sight.

For a while, we had a wonderful family down the street from Brazil, and when they moved in, that had very few possessions. The father was in Austin to finish his post doc work, and they were going to be living in Austin for just a few years. When Tim caught wind of this news, he delivered a dining table and chairs, a full set of dishes, pans to cook, and all kinds of kitchen utensils.

We became close friends with this family, and for New Year's, we invited them over and had a little party in the backyard, and Tim roped off Vietnam with these really cool long white bits of heavy-duty fabric so nobody had to look at it while the festivities took place. I named the "nice" side of the yard Miami.

Here's the deal. Everyone wants to be in Miami, but Vietnam is part of the package. As someone who enjoys a much more tidy and organized environment, Vietnam has been the source of a lot of anxiety for me, and for others who see it and can't wrap their heads around the clutter. Tim's taken great measures to clean it all out on a few occasions but it typically ends up going back to Vietnam status within a few weeks.

I failed to mention that in addition to collecting small things, Tim also collects extremely large things, like cars and boats. Currently, we own a Volkswagen Eurovan that doesn't run, a blue 1980's model Chevy Truck, a motorcycle or maybe two (I easily lose count because I don't travel to Vietnam often), a 2013 diesel SUV for my daily driving, and Emily Rose's 1984 Jeep Wagoneer. There are also three boats. *I know.* Not one, but three boats. Because you can never have enough boats that don't run!

At the end of the day, while the weird piles of things drive me crazy, I'm thankful that the bulk of the collection in Vietnam stays in Vietnam. I also remind myself that Tim has a plan for everything he buys, and that his collecting habit is so much better than an addiction to Fantasy Football or hookers. His habit isn't really even expensive since most of what he buys and collects is nearly free.

So Vietnam will remain. But I'll stay in Miami as much as I possibly can.

Talking to Fat People Around Fat People

Since I've been struggling with my weight for years, when it comes to talking about weight issues, I get very holier than thou and unapologetic about it. I feel I've earned the right to pass out advice to my thinner friends about how to handle talking to fat people about being fat. Under most circumstances—and I'm talking about at least 90% of the time—if you are talking to a person who is fat, you shouldn't talk to them about the fact they are fat unless they invite you to do so. You should also not talk about yourself and refer to yourself as fat around your friend who clearly outweighs you by 40 pounds.

Let me help you by taking it out of context for a minute for the sake of the lesson. Let's say you're friends with a unicorn, and you and the unicorn have never talked about the fact that she has a horn sticking out of her head. It's never come up because perhaps the unicorn doesn't want to talk about it, or perhaps, the unicorn feels embarrassed by the fact that she has a horn sticking out of her head, even though you both know it's there. So one night, you go to dinner together, make some small talk about your day, and then suddenly you have a burning need to discuss your forehead.

"Oh my GOD I am so frustrated by the zit on my forehead!" you say, pointing at it. "It's poking right out of the middle of my head. Look at it! It's terrible. I don't know how people go around dealing with things sticking out of their heads."

Meanwhile, how is your unicorn friend feeling? Pretty bad, I'd say.

The same goes for asking people if they are pregnant when you're not certain. Sadly, this often coincides with a person being fat. It's happened to me more than once. The first time, Emily Rose was around two years old and we were sitting in mass. I'd been part of the church choir for a while, but I'd given it up when the post partum depression knocked me out for the first year. On the Sundays when I could drag myself to church, Tim and I would sit with Emily Rose on one of our laps until she got too wiggly and needed to go back to the Time Out section in the glass room with the other exhausted parents and wiggly kids.

One Sunday at communion, as the choir was passing by, one of the older women in the choir who was rumored to be a bit of a drinker spotted us sitting in the pew and leaned over to admire Emily Rose. I was wearing a white blouse that was gathered right under the boobs, and my two-year post partum tummy poked out below the gathering. The woman gave me a quick once over and leaned in, pointed at my belly and whisper-yelled, "Do you have an announcement to make?"

I still die just thinking about it.

"No, I'm just fat.." I began, knowing I would burst into tears at any minute.

And then Emily Rose saved the day.

"I SMELL WINE!" she yelled.

And I'm sorry that I'm making fun of a sad woman with a bit of a drinking issue, but when Emily Rose said it, everyone around us started laughing, and suddenly, it wasn't about the sad drunk woman asking if I was pregnant (which was totally a reasonable question), it was eclipsed by the fact that my toddler so easily recognized the smell of wine. Aw, yeah.

It didn't stop then, though. Years later, Tim and I were on a road trip, and we stopped into a convenience store for gas, and they had one of those delis with those ridiculous potato wedges and some really kickass looking fried chicken, so of course we ordered some because that's just what you do on road trips (and why I am no longer high school skinny). As a sweet old woman behind the counter fetched our order, she looked at me and around to the side and said, "When are you due, baby?"

Oh, I was prepared for this. I'd had this one loaded up for some time.

"I'm not pregnant," I said rather loudly. "I'm JUST FAT. Also, I'm 43 years old, so it would basically be a miracle birth."

At which point, there was an audible gasp among the other patrons in the store.

"Well," she said (and not particularly remorseful, I might add), "We're in the country, baby. Everybody's here's pregnant."

Fair enough, but still. I couldn't let it go there.

"Well, it's a good day to learn a new life lesson," I said, "Never,

ever ask a woman if she's pregnant unless 1) she tells you she's pregnant or 2), you see a human head coming out of her vagina."

At the mere mention of the word "vagina," the men in the store did that thing that men do when someone enters the room with a hand grenade or a woman announces she's on her period. They all just scattered like oil in water to the far ends of the room. It was awesome.

Don't bother to ask me if I took this as an opportunity to pass up small town gas station fried chicken and potato wedges. I just scarfed it all down while I sobbed in the car and called that poor woman every terrible name in the book.

I grew up a beanpole, and had a taste of an eating disorder in high school that was never diagnosed by a professional, but I stayed high school skinny by alternating between a dedicated SlimFast regimen and that terrible three-day 1980s diet that included canned beets and vanilla ice cream. For a while, my idea of a balanced diet was having a Diet Coke for breakfast followed by a greasy white roll from the high school cafeteria, another Diet Coke, and canned green beans for dinner with another Diet Coke. The majority of my caloric intake took place on the weekends at keg parties where I consumed Bartles & Jaymes wine coolers purchased from our hometown bootlegger. I was super healthy.

Given all of these brilliant nutritional choices, I spent most of high school hovering around 125. There was a brief period where I thought adding Dexatrim to that mix made a lot of sense. Luckily, my mom busted me for that and so I went back to the Diet Coke and green beans. All of this eventually caught up with me, but I didn't become a fat person until my early 20s, when my metabolism got shot from contracting mono in Berlin when I was an exchange student. It was a pretty awful situation. I was hospitalized in a foreign country with very few people who spoke English around me, so I was never fully aware of what was going on around me. When I finally got out of the hospital, I weighed 107 pounds. After that, I spent my first year of college in my home town to recover, at which point I lived on a diet of East Texas chicken fried steak and mashed potatoes smothered in white gravy with German beer for dessert. Needless to say, I packed on the pounds like nobody's business.

My weight continued to climb through the years, and though I dieted down to a few reasonable goal weights, I just never got back to high school skinny. After I had Emily Rose, I never lost the baby weight. She's well into her teens, and I still tell people I haven't lost the baby weight, because I'm not really lying about that.

People are very comfortable around me and always have been. For that reason, when I became a fat person, skinny people continued to talk to me like I was a skinny person still. They would complain about how they needed to shop because they had recently gained weight (when to me, it seemed like they really hadn't). They would talk about needing to work out more because of how fat they were. All while talking to someone who was at least 35 pounds heavier.

Finally, it hit me. It wasn't about me! It was about them! And then I began figuring out the various scenarios that would cause a thin person to discuss weight around a person who is not thin. So I started calling people out on it.

"Hey, you do realize you're complaining about being fat around someone who is actually fat?"

"But I don't think of you as fat!" they would say. And they seemed somewhat sincere in this response, and I actually allowed myself to believe it for a while, and then I realized what a steaming load of horse manure that response is. If I sat across the table drinking wine with a man with Coke bottle glasses and complained about how blind I was, would he believe it if I said,

"But I don't think of you as blind!"

Come on.

I pressed on, because it happens so frequently. In all fairness, this is what women talk about when they're together. It hardly ever happens that two women sit and talk over wine without someone discussing how they want to change their bodies. So I gave it another shot with a woman who runs between five to eight miles a morning and who doesn't have an extra inch of body fat to pinch anywhere on her body.

"When I'm talking about my weight, it really has nothing to do with you," she said. "I know that my idea of fat for myself is different than yours, but I am really not comparing us at all."

Okay, that is fair. Her response is actually what has allowed me to get to a more comfortable place having body image discussions with thin people. All in all, I'm at a much more comfortable place with my body image, which is why I'm okay with writing about any of this in the first place. I recognize fully that the times when I was feeling the worst were the times when these conversations were the hardest, but it's become clearer to me in my old age that when people are talking about their bodies, they are not talking about yours.

But there's a caveat here: The super thin woman who helped me see this from a healthier perspective is a very dear friend. If you happen to be thin and you're drinking wine with a new acquaintance and that person clearly weighs more than you, I would advise that you don't start complaining about how fat you are around them, because it can make them feel paranoid and bad about themselves and suddenly they are ordering a third glass of wine and some fried chicken and potato wedges. What I'm saying here is please try to get out of your own head and be more sensitive, especially when talking to unicorns.

The Hormone Doctor
with the Sullivan Nod

everal years after Emily Rose was born, a sense of over-whelm and fatigue set in again. I'd gotten past the postpartum depression, but something was off again. I couldn't drag myself out of bed and my Texas allergies were causing me to wander around in a fog. My sleep patterns were all over the place, so I would crash early and wake up in the middle of the night wide awake and frustrated. Late one night, I flipped on a local channel and an infomercial came on touting the numerous benefits of Hormone Replacement Therapy. Like any other impressionable sucker, I got caught up in the list of symptoms of hormone imbalance, and of course I checked all the boxes. I found myself completely transfixed, so I called the next day and set an appointment, certain that this investment in my health was a great idea.

I'm a feminist with a few exceptions that might make other feminists squeamish. I want equal pay, but I want my husband to kill bugs and take out the trash. I want my voice heard at a company staff meeting, but if I get a flat tire, I'd like a strong man to lean in and take care of that for me.

So, when it comes to going to the doctor, I bring Tim. It's not that I think I need a man to be with me when I go to the doctor, it's that I'm such a freaked out hypochondriac that I feel like when the doctor tells me I have two weeks to live, Tim can handle the details. I need Tim there because while the doctor is moving his mouth, all I'm hearing is, "You have two weeks. I'm so sorry."

As it turns out, taking your husband to the magic Hormone Replacement Therapy doctor's office in the fancy part of town aligns perfectly with their business plan. The office looks like a page out of Elle Decor, sparsely appointed and black and sleek, yet still inviting. Every woman working there is stunningly beautiful and it's difficult to tell if they are 45 or 23. (Pro tip: You can always look at their hands to figure it out.) All of the women wear black and speak softly and slowly to make you feel at ease.

The first step was a consultation with the intake woman, a fiery redhead with perfect makeup and the boobs of a 20-year-old. She sweetly invited Tim to come along for the ride. We followed her into a beautiful office with low lights and smooth jazz. We sat down and she launched into the consultation questions, logging them on an iPad while I kicked Tim under the table for staring at her chest. I noted her hands were 47.

"Have you experienced symptoms of PMS?" she said over her leopard print reading glasses.

"Perhaps you should ask this guy," I said, pointing to Tim, while he laughed his huge loud laugh.

She faked a smile and continued.

"Weight problems?"

"I think we all know that's fairly obvious."

She didn't get my sense of humor. She continued on, asking about fatigue, skin problems, mood swings, and then we got to the true business at hand.

"How is your sex drive?"

I responded that it was never really an issue, that we were good in the sex department, always have been. She marked down an answer, removed her glasses, looked directly at Tim and said,

"After I began HRT, my sex drive increased like crazy. My husband loved it! We find that husbands really love the results."

Now, you probably wonder why I didn't just get up and leave right then. Tim can smell a scam fifty miles away, but I was desperate to feel better, and everyone seemed so happy there that it seemed like a good idea for me to continue down the path.

We discussed food allergies and seasonal allergies, and they would run a super fancy schmancy and ridiculously expensive allergy panel on me that morning if we had the time. Tim sat in the waiting room ogling the office staff and reading GQ while I stripped nude from the waist up and let a woman in a tight black turtleneck prick my back with needles. I nearly chewed a hole in my hand to keep from howling in pain.

"Wow, baby! Your back is lighting up like a Christmas tree back here! You *definitely* have a problem with mold, chocolate, and red wine."

Great. Two of those things were essentially the only pleasure I had left in my life at that point, and we're not talking about mold.

After the allergy panel, we were invited back to the doctor's office. The doctor entered the room and I kid you not, his sexy office assistant pulled out his chair for him. I'm surprised he didn't enter with a theme song. For a guy with a wispy combover and Botox bumps, this guy definitely commanded a room. I checked out his hands to reveal his age, and was so distracted by the giant gold ring he wore that I was temporarily mesmerized. I sat waiting for him to screw it to one side while moon dust flew around the room and hypnotized us both into signing up for ten years of hormone replacement therapy.

Have you ever heard of the Sullivan Nod? My sister applied for a job as a waitress in her early 20s, and part of the training was to help the waitstaff practice the Sullivan Nod. It goes something like this.

Waitperson to naive patron: So, you're having the burger with blue cheese and a side salad. And you'll be having a side of sweet potato fries on the side?

The waitperson asks this question while nodding their head. Naive patron says yes. In other words, the Sullivan Nod is a manipulation tool whereby while the salesperson assumes the sale through nodding, the customer just says yes. This doctor with the crazy moon dust ring was with us for no more than five minutes, but in that period, he asked several questions where he the only reasonable answer was yes. He Sullivan Nodded me into the following responses:

Why yes, I did suffer from sleeplessness!

Why yes, I did feel like I was forgetting things!

Why yes, I would like to have more sex! So would my husband!

His parting advice, and quite frankly, the best thing I got out of the entire experience, was that I should walk several miles a day, and to walk slowly. His assessment was that you didn't have to get your heart rate to crazy heights, you just needed to move your body every day. He ended the session by essentially giving Tim one of those sporty bro handshakes where you bump chests, leaning in and whispering, "You're going to thank me for this, believe me!"

The doctor left in a puff of magic smoke and the fiery redheaded office assistant entered the room, flashed a bleached white smile at Tim, showed us the astronomical bill, and handed me a sleek folder with instructions. She went over what creams to rub on my inner thighs, what to do with the pig thyroid, when to put the allergy drops under my tongue, and what to do with the buffered Vitamin C, and by the time we got in the car I was hungry, confused, and exhausted. Now that I think about it, it's exactly what those charlatans had planned all along.

Out of desperation to feel better, I went through with several months of both the hormone therapy and the allergy therapy. I will tell you in all honesty that the allergy drops actually worked, so some of the investment was worth it on that side. From there, everything else was a complete flop. The testosterone cream I rubbed on my inner thighs made my inner thighs hairy where they weren't before, but that paled in comparison to the constant state of rage I felt after it started kicking in. I wasn't losing weight, but I could power lift an SUV if given the chance. The pig thyroid made my heart race, and the buffered Vitamin C just felt like I was taking a twice-daily Alka-Seltzer meal replacement that made me burp constantly.

The added bonus of great sex is the biggest joke of all. How can you have sex when you're rubbing your inner thighs with man cream, injecting small doses of mold under your tongue, and burping like a truck driver all day? When you feel like punching a hole in the wall, is that the best time to hop into bed and have sex? I'm pretty sure Tim was too afraid of me during that time to even consider making a move.

I decided to research what was happening with the doctor since I saw him over a decade ago, and I was curious if he's still officing in the fancy part of town and still getting suckers willing to fork over thousands of dollars to fund his Botox and gold jewelry. As it turns out, he's had medical licenses revoked in both Texas and California for issues related to drug and alcohol abuse. He's also been charged with failure to maintain adequate records, reporting inconclusive allergy tests as positive, and billing insurance companies for allergy treatments he had not performed. None of this comes as a surprise to me. I think fair punishment would be to leave him alone in a boxing ring with 15 of his hairy-thighed, testosterone-pumped patients. That would straighten him out in a jiffy.

Needless to say, I ended up stopping all of it. If you were to ask a child to draw a picture of the experience, it would be a rough drawing of a very angry me burning piles of cash in a large trash can while Tim sat on the sidelines with a sad expression on his face that says above it, "Where is the sex?"

What a complete waste of time and load of crap that experience was. I feel it's important to share this with you, because ladies, a guy pimping hormones and promising that your husband will be happy with the results is not going to fix your marriage. If you go to a doctor's office and the biggest part of their sales pitch is the satisfaction level of the person who *isn't even the patient*, take your hairless thighs and walk the hell out of there.

You're Telling Me We Have A Good Marriage?

Tim and I have a terrible time remembering our anniversary. When we got married, good family friends who are potters made us a beautiful pottery bowl with our wedding date carved on the bottom. We keep the bowl up high in a cabinet in our kitchen, and the joke is that every year, one of us will bust the other person pulling the cabinet down to look at the date, so the other person gets to say,

"Hey, wait a minute! You don't remember our anniversary?"

Or, other years, we'll both forget. Either way, we're not really hung up on the anniversary celebration anyway. What we think is even funnier is how somehow, with our close friend group and even others who have known us for years, there is a very odd perception that we are the couple who has the most solid relationship. Perhaps they are just telling us this to make us feel better, but we've chosen to believe them. Sometimes we just look at each other and laugh and say,

"How did WE become the model for a good marriage?"

Let's not sugarcoat things, marriage is freaking hard. It's the hardest thing ever except doing hand-to-hand combat, curing plagues, or raising kids. Tim and I have been together for 21 years and married for 17, and during that time we've gone through a few things that challenged the hell out of our marriage. First, we had some long stretches where Tim was unemployed and I was the breadwinner. He was never at any point a lazy, unemployed person. He's resourceful and much better than me about cooking and housework, but still, there were times when I got pretty resentful about our situation.

Then there were the years that I had a huge problem with jealousy. When you marry someone who wasn't quite divorced yet when you fell in love with him, there's a tendency to worry that he will leave you for a new model once you've lost your shine. Lucky for us, I was never really that shiny to begin with, but we shared the same political views, the same general ideas about religion, and we made each other laugh. However, there were times when the Green Monster of jealousy took over and I became a crazy person, convinced Tim was leaving me for the toothless grocery cashier or the 22 year-old college neighbor in a tube top who had constant car trouble. This is where good therapy comes in handy. We had a marriage therapist who knew I had jealousy issues and he peered over his glasses and said, "There is always going to be someone thinner, someone who is prettier, smarter, funnier, sexier than you. However, there isn't another you out there, and he chose you." Game point: Therapist.

Like most married couples, we've battled our fair share of financial woes. We're both pretty terrible about money. Weirdly, I'm the one who pays the bills and manages our money, despite the fact that Tim is the much more frugal one and would likely do a better job of it. My weird feminist ways make me extremely stubborn about wanting to be the financial person in the house. In the near future, we're going to need to have someone work us through those problems unless a few million of you help out and buy this book, but I do know that in times of financial stress, our marriage suffers.

Those are really our main issues. You might think we would fight about parenting matters, but for the most part, we're on the same page there. We also handle our 14 year age difference really well and it hardly causes problems for us. That's not to say that we haven't had to resort to therapy on more than one occasion, especially in the beginning. Due to our financial woes, at one point, the only therapy we could afford was the free kind doled out by my company's Employee Assistance Program. We got what we paid for, which is a big fat goose egg. We sat down on the dusty couch in the therapist's sad little beige office, and when he crossed his legs during one of his long lectures, we both noticed he had holes in his shoes. We sat through the first session working very hard not to laugh out loud, and when we got in the car, we realized that if we could both manage an entire therapy session without laughing at our therapist's shoes, we were probably doing okay.

Our most consistent couple's therapy came after I had a particularly difficult time with the Green Monster of Jealousy and we signed up for a six-week group therapy session in addition to our private courses. We dug in deep, and the group therapy worked wonders for us because we're competitive and wanted to win by staying married. We loved comparing ourselves to the more dysfunctional couples.

Years after the group therapy, Tim and I were having a date night at a literary reading in Austin. We were seated at a high bar table drinking beer, and our group therapist walked up. He didn't recognize us, but I said,

"Steve! We're the Arndts! Remember us?"

It took a second for things to compute, then Steve looked genuinely and sincerely surprised to see us together.

"We're still married!" I bragged while he stood there looking shocked.

"It's because we started drinking!" Tim said, pointing at his beer and Bert laughing. (Tim's not a big drinker.) It's possible that our joke was a little lost on Steve, who congratulated us for being together. I thanked him for helping us during our hardest times and he walked off, probably shaking his head and rolling his eyes.

Often, younger people ask us for advice on how to have a solid marriage. I often resist the urge to tell them that the key to a happy marriage is to offer up a sexual favor once a week, and to be consistent about that every single week of your marriage, because I have a friend who actually does that and I every time I think of it I want to laugh my head off and high-five her all at the same time. I'm certain her husband high-fives her on a regular basis. Someone needs to build a statue in her honor or give that woman a gold trophy and I'm not kidding.

For us, we have some pretty specific aspects of our relationship that we're convinced helps keep us married. It's different for everyone, but these things don't hurt:

You have to have trust. The cornerstone of our marriage is that we've established mutual trust. Despite my many years of issues with a massive jealous bone, I learned that if I can't trust Tim to respect our marriage, we will have constant fights and problems. So I learned to let my trust issues go, and with established mutual trust, we both feel lighter about things. I trust that Tim will be there for me when I need a soft spot to land. I trust that if I need a bug squashed, he'll step up and step on it. He trusts that if I say I'll pick up the kids at a certain time, it's happening. We keep our lines of communication open, and we sincerely trust each other.

It helps to the same political beliefs. I'm sorry, but even though I absolutely love James Carville and Mary Matalin, there is no way in hell I could sustain a long-term marriage with someone with opposite political views. I have a few friends who have husbands with whom they disagree politically, and it is not easy for them at all. Tim and I aren't on the same page about every detail, but overall, we're both bleeding heart lefties who want everyone to have enough food and would prefer we keep our borders open so everyone can join us in a huge liberal 21st century version of Hands Across America. I personally feel that at least *mostly* matching political views keep a marriage on a solid path, but that's just me.

You don't need fancy gifts to have a good marriage. We still wear our $27 sterling silver James Avery wedding rings. I didn't even own a diamond ring, engagement or otherwise, until last year when Tim gifted me with a simple diamond band that he bought second hand because God bless Tim Arndt, that is just how the man rolls. Fancy rings, as far as I know, haven't helped marriages last. Not that they aren't pretty and all, but have you seen *Blood Diamond?*

Years ago, before Emily Rose was born and Matthew and Stephanie were little, we ventured out for the 4th of July in downtown Austin to see the fireworks on the water. We brought along our canoe and blankets and food for picnicking, and we also brought along several friends. On the way home, Tim abruptly pulled over to the side of the road in a residential area, and the next thing you know, he's grabbing a huge cut-out of wood in the shape of a heart and strapping it to the top of the Suburban. I knew better than to ask questions.

The sign was propped on the side of our garage for months, and I completely forgot about it. Months later, I was working in sales at a software company that had a large sales floor with open cubes and a huge glass wall of windows facing the front of the building. It was Valentine's Day, and the day was going along like all normal days when I got up to go to the restroom, and when I walked back, everyone was standing up and looking at me, and people were buzzing with excitement. One of my coworkers ran up to me and said dramatically,

"Oh, Amy! Can you believe it?"

For just a brief minute, I wondered if someone died. At the same time, the receptionist came up with a huge vase of flowers and shoved them in my hand. Tim's birthday is on Valentine's Day, so he loves spending his birthday delivering flowers. He's also the kind of guy with a flair for the dramatic. As I approached my desk, everyone was pointing to the glass wall of windows, and there, propped up against the glass facing my desk was the huge wooden heart. On it, Tim had written:

I LOVE YOU.

Girls, let me tell you, that massive wooden heart was a million times better than the flowers. For one, every woman there was green with envy. I got so much attention it was kind of embarrassing. What was even better was that one of the men stood up and said,

"That bastard! We'll all spend hundreds of dollars on Valentine's Day and that schmuck shows up with a big piece of wood and some paint on it and everyone loses their mind."

You have to admit that is pretty great. Tim still laughs so hard about that, even the fact that he got in trouble from our Director of Facilities who was afraid his bold statement might break her windows, because I think she believed she actually owned the building. Less than $10 worth of paint and years later, people still talk about that Valentine's Day gift. Even better, years later, my stepson used the same sign to invite his then-girlfriend to prom. He waited outside on the street where she drove to school and when she approached the stop sign, there he was, peeking over the sign that clearly ends in good luck for the Arndt guys.

There you have it. Trust. Political Alignment. Inexpensive gifts. It works!

Is That a Pineapple in Your Cart?

My particular flavor of midlife crisis started with a huge wave of paranoia about getting osteoporosis, given that my grandmothers on both sides turned into tiny little humpbacked whale ladies in their golden years. To combat that, I started working on my strength and posture. I went to Barre classes where other middle-aged women with similar fears squeezed in with the young ones. Together, we would raise our screaming haunches up an inch and down an inch for an hour until we couldn't walk for days.

I got a FitBit. I decided that tracking my every move might inspire me to actually move. In the early days, it was pretty addictive, and if I had 200 steps to go before hitting my 10K goal, I'd mall-walk from our living room to the bedroom and back until it vibrated my congratulations. Once I realized how powerful the vibration mechanism was, I wondered why middle-aged women didn't wear their FitBits in their panties.

I also bought a convertible. It's totally cliche, but if the reason for getting a convertible is to get attention, it absolutely worked.

Like when I was pulling out of a coffee shop that I frequent, and a small brown man with a thick accent walked up and said, "I like you car. I like you, too." Instead of correcting his English, I checked to make sure he wasn't masturbating, and then I realized that he was just innocently appreciating a blonde woman in a convertible. I offered him a coy sideways beauty pageant wave and drove away feeling pretty great about life.

To be fair, I didn't go out and buy a brand spanking new yellow convertible. Tim, ever frugal, found a blue, single-owner 2001 BMW convertible from a woman transitioning out of *her* midlife crisis.

When Tim talks about buying the convertible, he tells everyone, "I bought it so she wouldn't get a cabana boy." Fair enough, given that I suddenly had potential play with men the size of cabana boys. I loved every minute driving it during the two months in Austin when the weather allowed for it. The rest of the year, I commandeered Tim's big SUV and let him cram inside the convertible because he's a saint and I was having "perimenopausal" warm moments.

One morning after writing at the coffee shop, I was driving home in the convertible with the top down. I had on my Lululemon leggings that cost about as much as the car, and my hair was in the kind of ponytail that doesn't say "I give up." The ponytail said, "I'm free, happy, and I worked at this." In other words, I was feeling pretty darned good about myself. I was probably singing along to Drake like all the cool moms.

I exited onto the feeder road of the interstate when a guy in a black SUV pulled up next to me, rolled down his window, and motioned for me to slow down. He had on really dark sunglasses, a black t-shirt, and a little love patch of facial hair poking out underneath his lip. (This is the exact description I would provide to the police if I had to draw a sketch.) This was all happening while navigating a feeder road at 40 mph, but for just a brief minute I began to think this random man in dark sunglasses was checking me out. I couldn't blame him.

At second glance, I realized it was the husband of one of my friends that I haven't seen in forever. He's the lead singer of a successful touring band, and I don't keep up with what car he drives, so it took me a minute to figure it out, and then he yelled,

"Pull over, Amy!"

I changed lanes and got behind him and followed him into the back parking lot of the In-N-Out Burger that's a few blocks from my house. We got out of our cars to greet each other, and as he approached me, I started apologizing.

"Mark! I am SO embarrassed. I didn't realize it was you and just for a second, I thought you were just a random guy hitting on me!"

This is when things got weird. The man walked up and stood right in front of me and said,

"I saw that convertible and saw you in it, and I got *real* horny."

It was at that moment when I realized that this guy wasn't my friend Mark. Mark would never in a million years say that, much less say "real" instead of "really." At that point, I was halfway terrified of getting raped at the In-N-Out Burger, but because I'm having a midlife crisis and was feeling pretty cute that day, I was also a little giddy and flattered. It was an odd mixture of emotions driven primarily by fear.

"Oh, oh my goodness. You're not Mark. I am so sorry. I thought you were my friend's husband. You must think I'm crazy that I pulled over. I am so sorry!" I began stepping backwards, trying to weave my keys in between my fingers in the old college self-defense trick where you stab a guy in between the eyes with your keys. Has that move ever actually worked?

"You like to party?" he asked, stepping in a little closer.

"Oh, I do," I said, stepping backwards again. "With my HUSBAND. In the privacy of OUR OWN HOME." I wondered if I was about to be the set-up for a gruesome Lifetime movie called "The Convertible Murders."

"I'm a married mom with kids!" I went on, "I am so sorry, I really thought you were a friend of mind. This is all just a huge misunderstanding. You look EXACTLY like my friend's husband who's the lead singer of a band. I mean, it's uncanny..."

"Where's your spirit of adventure?" he asked, smiling. "You know what they say about missed opportunities."

I couldn't think of anything witty to say at that moment, but later really wished I'd told him that I couldn't quite recall when I'd last showered, so he might really want to miss that "opportunity," but instead, I scurried back in the car and drove off while he shrugged and walked back to his love shack on wheels. I was a little bit hysterical, frozen in a moment of being completely terrified and guilty, embarrassed for being so stupid to follow a stranger I thought was a friend, but experiencing some joy for still having "it." I patted my convertible lovingly for doing its job.

As I drove off, I had a lot of racing thoughts. *Didn't he say, "Pull over, Amy?" I guess he must have said, "Pull over, baby!" He must have thought I was down to party! I mean, I followed him into the In-N-Out parking lot for God's sakes! And what if I had just gone for it? Can you imagine that scene? Sweaty middle-aged woman piles in the back of a stranger's SUV while innocent families are ordering burgers at In-N-Out just a few feet away? His Faith No More CD sets the mood. They start "partying." It's a tight squeeze in there, but somehow the strange man manages to take off the middle-aged woman's panties and much to his surprise, a FitBit falls out.*

I tried to convey the humor of this to Tim, but he didn't exactly appreciate the thought of his wife painting the picture of a daytime tryst behind the In-N-Out Burger. He didn't even appreciate the humor of my sad joke about a little "in and out at the In-N-Out." Mainly, he was relieved that nothing terrible happened because he's a really great husband.

A few weeks passed, and I was once again donning leggings and a decent ponytail while shopping in the bulk foods section of my neighborhood grocery store. I get anxiety in grocery stores because of the combination of fluorescent lighting and overwhelming choices, so I usually stick in my headphones, arming myself with some smooth jazz to get me through it. On this particular morning, the grocery was relatively empty, so I was feeling okay. As I moved my cart to the lentil area, a tall, tan man with salt and pepper hair stood filling up a baggie of peppered cashews. I'm the kind of person who smiles at people in grocery stores, so I smiled at the man and went on about my lentil seeking. I made my way over to the canned tomato aisle where I was hunched over my cart reading a recipe on my phone and talking to myself like I do when suddenly, I felt a hand. On my HIP.

It was a quick brush, but it was absolutely a person touching my hip. I looked up quickly and there was the tan man with the salt and pepper hair, looking sheepish while we both said, "I'm sorry."

I don't know why I apologized to him for him touching my hip, but given the size of my hips, I guess I felt like they were in his way.

He moved on down the empty aisle and began picking up merchandise at the end of the aisle while I stood there in a state of shock pondering what just happened. Was that an accident? Was it on purpose?

It was at that moment when I realized that the man had a pineapple in his cart. It was at that moment that I began taking pictures of the man. I had to document this! If you're like I was for most of my life, you don't know about the pineapple in the cart and what it supposedly represents. My girlfriend who's in real estate knows a lot of these urban legends, and she swears that in one particular Austin suburb, if a person places a pineapple in their cart, it means they are, for lack of a better phrase, "down to party." It also indicates that the person flashing a pineapple is down to party with other spouses. *Swingers!*

After I took a few clandestine pics of Pineapple Guy, I decided to test him to see if he was really making a move on me. You know how you get on the same path with someone in the grocery you end up bumping into them every aisle until at some point you laugh and say, "Fancy meeting you here?" I wasn't risking that with Pineapple Guy, so I made a beeline for the butter area way across the store. I waited in the cold dairy area excited at this odd game of Middle-Aged Cat and Mouse. And before I could make a determination of whether I wanted salted or unsalted butter, there he was at the end of the aisle. It was SO intentional!

I wish I'd had bigger ovaries and just talked to him to find out what he wanted, but I chickened out and scurried away, exiting via the pet food aisle in case I needed a cat lady or two to come to my defense. As I waited at the checkout, my adrenaline pumped, knowing at any minute he might appear. It was that same feeling of mild disgust and mild flattery that I'd experienced on In-N-Out Day.

This may seem odd to admit, but I understand why people have full blown midlife crises and do crazy things like jump out of planes or get matching ZZ Top tattoos with their cousins. There's something poignant about reaching midlife and wondering what could you have done differently and what are you still going to do. At some point when midlife hits, you look in the mirror and wonder what happened to the skin under your eyes or what happened to your skin under your upper arms or what happened to pretty much all of your skin. As things on our bodies move around and change, that's scary for most of us. I found an entire new section of my ass that's just about a half an inch below where the base of my ass should be. That's the kind of stuff that sends you straight to Sono Bello for a complimentary consultation.

Part of this period in life makes you wonder why you don't get hit on like you did in your 20s and 30s, so that when a nice looking guy in the grocery spots you and weirdly touches your hip, you briefly wonder what it might be like to follow through with whatever both of you have in mind. That's when I use my imagination to laugh myself out of taking action, because I know what it would be like. Just like my vision of what the In-N-Out Burger scene would have really been like, I imagine going home and telling Tim that we have a date with a couple who live in the suburbs, and on Friday night, we're going to try swinging for the first time, and then I just laugh so hard thinking about Tim's face that I realize I can't even think about it again.

Lucky for me, I remain madly in love with Tim, and still completely attracted to him, so I don't need a pineapple in someone else's cart to keep the spark going. We have enough spark on our own, thank you very much, and it's on our own time in our own house (or, when we're feeling feisty about every five years, Pease Park, but again, that's supposed to be a secret).

In an ironic twist of fate, the doohickey that opens the lid to the convertible decided to quit working, and a few weeks later the A/C decided to stop as well, so we ended up selling the BMW to a neighbor from Saudi Arabia who I think used it to pick up chicks. Circle of life.

I Really Can't Wait to Get Old

When you grow up with two extremely glamorous grandmothers who had closets filled with matching handbags and shoes and lots of clip-on earrings, you kind of can't wait to get old. I spent hours and hours in Granny Underwood's closet, wearing her silver platform heels, putting on red lipstick at her fluorescent-lit makeup mirror that had four settings (evening pink was the best). She let me take long, luxurious baths in her fancy bathtub with the gold fixtures. I would smell like Neutrogena soap and cigarette smoke for days and I loved it. For me, getting old meant having unlimited access to Dr Pepper, driving giant cars, and playing golf, which I guess in some cases is true.

Granny Underwood was a nurse, and later a head administrator of the nursing home in her small Texas town, so from an early age, I hung out with the old people and was totally comfortable with that. Rumor has it one Christmas I stepped up on a chair at a holiday party at the nursing home and belted out "Jingle Bells" to entertain the old people. Where was YouTube when I needed it?

I loved the old people at my Granny's nursing home, like the woman who had no filter who would sit outside her room in her wheelchair and if she thought you were ugly, would simply shout,

"You're ugly!"

Old people get to do that for some reason. They can say anything with zero filter and even though it might not feel great to be on the receiving end of that, you can't deny it's funny as hell.

My Grandma Mabel was equally funny, and since she was old when I was little, I got the idea in my head that being old was a really cool thing. Grandma cussed like a sailor, and had huge breasts that she pretended were a burden, but she actually adored the attention she got from them. When we would get in the car, we had to remind her to wear a seatbelt because it wasn't a law when she drove, and she would sigh dramatically and say,

"I hate seatbelts. They make me feel like a big tit wrapped up in a brassiere."

I remember one time my BFF Christi Cole was over when Grandma made that comment, and I thought Christi might faint on the spot. Grandmas weren't supposed to say words like "tit." Grandma said all of the words you weren't supposed to say, which is why she was so much fun. She also burped with reckless abandon, and called her burps "The Bots." She would burp and burp and shrug and say,

"Sorry. I've got 'The Bots.'" And we would fall over laughing.

Since Grandma got away with it, I figured getting old was just license to say what you want and burp without getting in trouble. Of course, now that I'm actually getting older, some of the things about aging aren't exactly delightful. Just recently I began checking my make-up in my car mirror when I realized that my neck is starting to look like skin-colored tissue paper. I'm not exactly loving that. I'm guessing next, it will be hemorrhoids?

Despite these frustrations, I still see a lot of glamour in aging. One summer at a resort in Mexico, I spotted a woman in a bright green floral one-piece bathing suit with bright pink and orange flowers on it. It was a super loud suit that said, "Look at me!" She looked to be about 80, and with her fabulous bathing suit, she was wearing bright orange lipstick. She was one of those old ladies who's tan but doesn't look like a leather satchel, as if she tanned just the right amount of time for every one of her 80 years on Earth. She wasn't thin, and didn't have the kind of body society wants traipsing around in a swimsuit at a resort, but she didn't give one single shit, and didn't even bother wearing a cover-up. I couldn't take my eyes off of her to the point where Emily Rose told me to quit being rude and staring, but I just wanted to soak in the exact look I want when I'm that age.

I love a floral one-piece, but I absolutely die for a caftan. Not a muumuu; a proper caftan. I feel like elderly women get to wear them daily and nobody cares, but doing that at my age would raise eyebrows, and for good reason. I have a lovely purple caftan that my friend bought on a trip to Morocco, and I wear it more often than I should admit. When I get old enough, I may wear it every day. The caftan makes me want to play Mahjong. I've tried a few times to get a weekly Mahjong game going a few times, and everyone looks at me like I'm 92. So I am looking forward to being 92 so someone will play Mahjong with me.

One thing I'm not certain about is sex when you're elderly.

I have a good friend who has a much larger spirit of adventure than me, and she told me this crazy story about how she went on a date with a man she met online who said he was in his early 50s but ended up being closer to 75. She sat down and got a good look at him and was pissed at first, then she decided to just enjoy talking with him since it clearly wasn't going to be a love match. As the discussion went on, the man revealed that he feels he has to change his age because he *feels* much younger than he is, and in a way, I sympathize. I'm 47 and I feel 26 and I think I always will. Before she died, my mother-in-law used to say that she would look in the mirror and say,

"Who is that old woman?"

In her head, she felt like she was still in her 20s. I get that.

So this old man was talking to my friend about a number of fascinating topics, when he revealed that he attends these workshops that are designed to celebrate and I guess maximize the female orgasm. I know, the idea is weird coming from an old man, but hang in here with me. He proceeded to tell my friend that in these workshops, it's designed for couples and they're all in a big room, and the partners, most of whom are men, are instructed to lightly touch the woman's clitoris for thirteen minutes.

You heard me, THIRTEEN minutes.

When my friend told me this, the first thing out of my mouth was,

"Can I have his number?"

Then we laughed for about thirteen straight minutes. After we quit laughing, I had about a million questions. Did she consider going? Nope. Too weird, even for her (she admits she is weird).

Did other people watch? She didn't really know. Did this lovely little favor get reciprocated? Nope, it appeared to be focused solely on the female orgasm. I asked 200 more questions, then raced home to tell Tim all about it. Given that Tim and I can hardly do anything for thirteen minutes without falling dead asleep, and there's no chance in hell I'm going to whip out my body part in front of a roomful of strangers, let's just say that we didn't end up signing up to try it out.

On the flipside, I am excited about getting old and doing things that aren't age-appropriate. Take dancing, for example. I am more interested in dancing than I ever was in my 20s or 30s, and I expect to enter my golden years dancing like a mofo. I already drive about 37 in the fast lane, so I'm looking forward to slowing down to about 17. As I age, I'm less and less afraid to express my opinion, so I can't wait to start telling people they're ugly. I'm already experimenting with orange lipstick.

It's a start.

Oh Yeah, About Al Roker

emember how I dedicated this book to the friends with whom I'd ride to El Paso and Al Roker? Have you been wondering why I brought up Al Roker and never addressed it until now? Please go ahead and pat yourself on the back for reading this entire book and for your patience, because that was my evil plan all along.

At long last, it's time for you to learn about my mild obsession with Al Roker.

I love Al Roker for a long list of reasons. I would give anything to ride to El Paso with Al Roker! He's constantly jovial. He lost over 100 pounds after having gastric bypass surgery in 2002, and for the most part, he keeps it off. I think that's rather impressive given that it takes me two years to lose five pounds. He's madly in love with his beautiful wife Deborah Roberts, and a great dad to his three kids. He's second cousins with Lenny Kravitz!

Al is very active on Twitter and pushes back on his trolls in the most clever of ways. When a troll mentioned that he would no longer watch the *Today Show* because of Al Roker, Al simply replied, "We'll miss you though not quite sure what you're talking about." Or, when a troll accused Roker of tweeting "more 'Demorat' propaganda," Roker replied, "Or you could just watch and judge for yourself, or at least consult a dictionary." Al is dedicated to educating us about climate change, despite what anti-science trolls have to say about it.

"Climate change affects everybody," Al said in a recent *Today Show*" blog. "It doesn't care if you're black or white, rich or poor, male or female. Climate change affects everybody, and the notion that we can ignore it is just foolhardy. We are talking about the fate of our planet."

Speaking of our planet, you'd have to be living under a giant iceberg not to have heard about Al having a little bowel-related accident in the White House after his gastric bypass. Al was at the White House on assignment when he felt the need to pass gas. He did, but due to the side effects of the surgery, likely combined with something that he ate, and poor Al gambled and lost.

"I was panicking, so I got to the restroom of the press room, threw out the underwear and just went commando." Al told Dr. Nancy Snyderman in a 2013 *Dateline* interview.

Remember how I peed my wedding dress, stripped off my spanks and went on about my wedding night? I forgot to mention that I continued on with my wedding reception completely commando. And perhaps about 57 times since my wedding, I've done the same thing. Anyone knows me knows that I pee my pants with regularity, but now you also know that I throw away underwear like they're disposable.

Al and I are kindred spirits is what I'm saying here. I love that man!

I've been to New York several times in the past few years for work or pleasure trips, and each time I made a point to stop by the Today Show Plaza with the hopes of seeing him. I've actually seen him in the flesh twice, but haven't gotten close enough to actually shake his hand or pummel him with my body for a massive hug. One of the times I went to see him, he was out of sorts about the lighting and one of the interns told me it wasn't the best day to try to meet him. Of course I was crushed. I need Al to be in a very good head space when he meets me.

I'm probably on some kind of list for the weirdo fans that the *Today* cast has to watch out for, but I'm not giving up. My dream for many, many years has been to write a book and talk about that book on the *Today Show*, and of course during that time, I want some face time with Al to thank him for being so awesome and for being one of my favorite people. Since one of those has finally come true, I'm optimistic that I'll meet Al in due time. I'm a firm believer that if you dream hard enough and work just as hard, it will happen.

Here's to seeing you soon, Al!

Knitting a Sweater and Creating World Peace

For many years, our family's New Year's Eve tradition has been to invite over a small group of friends to eat fondue, drink champagne, and make vision boards. The vision boards started with a simple idea from my friend Candace to start the year off with a positive note. I liked the idea because I knew a woman who made a vision board with a fancy elaborate swimming pool, and in just a few years, she actually built that fancy elaborate swimming pool. I liked the idea that focusing on your vision could help it actually happen.

I'm a weird combination of being overly optimistic yet cautiously realistic at the same time, so when I have a list of goals, I like to make it big so that I accomplish something and if things fall off, so be it. For that reason, I often tell Tim the list of things I have on my plate for the day, and I always end the list the same way,

"Okay, Tim, today I'm going to take Emily Rose to the dentist, drop her back off at school, run to the coffee shop and write for a few hours, run to Home Depot for some more landscaping stones, come home, work through some yard work, clean the kitchen, fold some laundry, take a nap, go to yoga, write some thank-you notes, knit a sweater, and create world peace."

Tim knows exactly what this means. I will never get to the sweater-knitting, mainly because as I mentioned earlier I really hate crafts, but also, my lists are always so ambitious it feels like I might as well knit a full sweater and create world peace before I fall into bed, completely satisfied with my time management and ability to do it all in one day.

But this is real life, so typically, it ends up looking something like this. I take Emily Rose to the dentist, but we're 15 minutes late because she dawdled doing Lord knows what on the way to the school office, and also due to Austin's horrible traffic,which makes me say incredibly vulgar things to strangers driving either a Prius or a Ford F150 because we all recognize that 99% of all traffic problems are due someone driving a Prius or a Ford F150.

I sign in at the reception desk, sweating and shaking from my massive road rage. I knock out some emails and some Words With Friends while we're at the dentist, then drop Emily Rose off at school, realizing when we pull up to the school that we forgot the dentist's note and her absence will be unexcused until we work that out, so I drive back to the dentist, cussing at myself for wasting another hour of the day when I should have been writing.

The day continues on like this and I skip the writing time, don't go anywhere near a thank-you note, completely ignore the yard work/yoga/laundry plans, opting to prioritize the nap above all else because, hey, self-care is really important. Perhaps this run-down of how I manage my time will explain why it's taken me five years to write this book.

Still, every single vision board I've ever made includes the word "book" on it. It's been the single consistent goal in my life for years and years. Since I was eight, I've fantasized about what it would be like to hold a book I've written in my own hands. As a generality, I have a simple set of goals: Write the book, hold the book in my hands, talk about that book on *Today*. To me, all of these things seem pretty doable. They may say I'm a dreamer?

I've expanded on this fantasy by thinking about being in an airport and seeing my book on the stands in the airport bookstore. I've actually gone into bookstores and taken selfies at the bookshelves, pretending in my head that I'm standing there posing with my book. Perhaps my book is right next to Mike Tyson's tattoo book, or Stormy Daniels' cookbook. I really don't care!

In my more elaborate airport fantasy, I take a comfortable seat in the Amerian Airlines Admirals Club to board my flight to Bora Bora when I notice a woman reading my book. She's well dressed and savvy, and she picked up my book at the airport bookstore that morning. Of course, since it's my fantasy and I get to create the rules here, her layover was so long that when I happen onto her, she's on the last page of my book and she is wiping away tears and laughing. She takes a deep breath to let it all soak in, then turns to the person next to her and says, "You HAVE to read this. I laughed and cried like I haven't laughed and cried in ages!"

The person next to her accepts the book without question and opens it up, starts reading, and cracks a big smile.

That man is Al Roker.

Do you see how this all comes full circle? I really love this story, even if it is completely made-up, because I believe that if I build it, even in my weird middle-aged adult woman fantasy, it will come.

I am a firm believer that it is never too late to live your dreams. I say it often because I believe it wholeheartedly. My family has been through a ton of ups and downs to arrive at the place where I can hold a book that I wrote in my hands because I never gave up on that dream.

So, I'd like to challenge you to do the same. Go make your dreams happen!

Learn the ukulele. Jump out of the plane (but please take the safety courses first!). Write the letter to your dad who quit talking to you in 1987. Take the cooking class! Book the trip. Engage in the political debate, even if it makes you uncomfortable. Be willing to be a human chunk of Play-Doh and let yourself be molded into many different shapes and forms.

Grab the right person and pack up a car for a long road trip.

Might I suggest El Paso?

Acknowledgments

One of my favorite things in the world is the carnival ride that's a big rocking ship that takes you super high and drops you in a free-fall back and forth until you're bright red in the face from fear or laughter or a lovely combination of both. When I was little, the rocking ship at Six Flags over Texas in Arlington was called "The Conquistador," so I call all variations of the ride by that name. To this day, if I have a chance to go to a roadside carnival or an amusement park, I make a beeline for The Conquistador.

Writing the acknowledgments for this book makes me feel like I'm about to ride The Conquistador. It makes me giddy with excitement to get to the place where this book is finally ready, and I can thank the large list of people who helped me get here.

I wouldn't have started this book without the encouragement of my absolutely incredible friend Candace, whom I've been friends with since 7th grade. In 2013, Candace texted me a photo of the cover of Glennon Doyle's book *Carry On, Warrior* and told me that I should write a book of my own. She let me borrow the book, and I read it in about two days and left it on my bedside table to encourage me. Six years later, I still have the book on my bedside, and my book is finally a reality. Candace, thank you for the countless nights talking through ideas and dreams, for being with me during the dark times and the celebrations, and for being the world's best listener. I guess you can have your book back now!

Endless thanks to Lori, Amy, Amy, and Joanne. Your friendships and encouragement mean more to me than I can express. I love that I have my Lori and Candace group and my Amy, Amy, and Joanne group, and that we each have our own lovely individual friendships as well. You are so important to me. I love you all.

To Kirk and Rasha: What would I do without our group texts and your love? Thank you for putting up with me all of these years.

To the BFHs: You know who you are! Thank you for many, many years of friendship and group texts, and for staying friends with me despite the years where I was flaky.

To the Cole family - to Linda and Jerry for being second parents to me, to Doug for attempting to toughen me up by shooting me with a BB gun (news flash: it didn't work), and to Christi for being the best childhood friend in the world. I love you, Cole family!

To Dr. Blevens, the professor who pushed me the hardest and continues to encourage me 20 years later, thank you for helping me believe I had it in me.

To Russel Secker: Thank you for reaching out to talk about publishing options, and for your support and encouragement. I've admired you for so many years!

To Olga Campos Benz: I'm so thankful we met at the Writer's League conference so long ago and that we've maintained a friendship ever since. Your book inspired me to finish mine. I'm looking forward to our next round of margaritas at Manuel's.

To Kelly Willis: Thank you for so effortlessly saying yes. You continue to blow me away with your talent and grace!

To Trasi: You're such an incredibly supportive friend, you came to my event after having car trouble. Most people would have gone home. You're a keeper.

Speaking of Trasi, to Trasi, Kelsey, Lisa, and Trish - thank you for the monthly pep talks at our Hyde Park Mom's happy hours. Love you gals!

To Spike Gillespie: I'm so glad that you wrote that wonderful magazine piece in the 90s (that I still need to have you sign!), then decades later, you graciously invited me to come to the Tiny T Ranch to learn how to officiate a wedding. Thank you for bringing me into writing group, and for letting me test out chapters out loud. Your advice has been priceless to me.

To Phil West: Thank you for your editing work, and for not throwing in the towel despite having to read the word "vagina" countless times. You hung in there like the champ you are!

To Alex Lloyd: From the time you invited me to room with you our work trip to our long dinners with laughter and tears, I've loved you to pieces. Thank you for your keen eye and for doing the final edits!

To Drue Wagner: You get me! Your cover design still gives me chills. It's perfect. Thank you for your hard work and your talent.

To Tiffany Harelik: Thank you for your expert advice and help with the publishing process. I absolutely couldn't have finished this project with your sage advice and organizational skills!

To the staff at Cherrywood Coffeehouse: For the countless coffees with plenty of room for cream, American breakfasts, and kohlrabi salads with blackened catfish, thank you for being my home away from home. Thank you for the hugs and encouragement along the way. Cherrywood is forever my good luck writing space.

To Priscilla, my lifesaver. When I had doubts about writing, you said, "There will be other books, but nobody can write your story." Of course you were right.

Sister Emily/Emily Mouse/Thupa Squirrel/Tia: Before anyone else knows, you know. Besides our parents and Stevie Wonder, you are the person I've loved the longest. Thank you for letting me write about Feek. For what it's worth, your stories are the most important to me. Thank you for being there with me every step of the way.

To Pam: Thank you for loving us before you met us. You taught me how to be a stepmother, and because of you, I think I got pretty good at it. You are an example of what pure love looks like. I love you so much!

To Dad: Thank you for truly coming around to texting! Thank you for the countless detailed messages when I needed background information, and for sharing so much about your past with me. I'm endlessly thankful that you opened up about the good times and the rough times, and for your wit and sense of humor. I like to think you passed some of that down to me. Also, thanks for not spray painting me burnt orange. I love you.

On my wall at my desk is a hand-written note from my step-father James that says, "I hope you write that book. I hope you get it published. I hope you can talk about it on *The Today Show*." So many times when I felt stalled during the writing process, I turned to that note. James, the last time I read a chapter to you, you smiled with a twinkle in your eyes and said, "You are so good!" I believed you. Thank you for that.

To Mom: From your Fruit Cocktail Reading Program to your never-ending support and encouragement, I'll never be able to thank you adequately for keeping me going my entire life. I can call you any hour, any day, any place, and you will take the call. I think you love me so much, there have been times you've wanted this book more than I have. You always bring me back and keep me moving. I love you always.

To Matthew and Stephanie: What a priceless gift you have both been to me! Thank you both for welcoming me into your lives from such an early age, and for teaching me how to be a mother. I'm so proud to be your stepmother and I love you both so much.

To Emily Rose/ER/Rosie/Rosie Bosie: From the moment I knew you were coming into the world, I've loved you fiercely and unconditionally, and that love continues to grow every day. Thank you for our big talks, our mutual trust, our shared love of fashion and good movies, and our dinner dates. You made our family whole.

To Tim: Only recently did you tell me that when I address you as "Tim Arndt" you think it's weird, so I decided to just address this to you by your first name, and I'm not gonna lie; it feels very uncomfortable to do that. Anyway Tim Arndt, how many times have you told me to go for it and finish this book?

I could search the world over and never find a more patient and encouraging partner in crime. Thank you for killing the bugs, for lifting the heavy things, for fixing the cars and things, for finding Mont Blancs, and for listening to every chapter (some more than once). The best is yet to be.

CPSIA information can be obtained
at www.ICGtesting.com
Printed in the USA
LVHW042325290820
664253LV00004B/368